Contents

Acknowledgments

I should like to thank Henny Kormelink and Egbert van Hes for allowing me to bring their "De Kartotheek" to North America and Roger Bongaerts, Director of The Dutch Soccer Academy, for his many hours translating and facilitating the drills.

Cover photography courtesy of Empics Sports Photo Agency. Matthew Ashton, Photographer.

Cover Design by Phil Velikan.

Dutch Soccer Drills

Volume 1: Individual Skills

Richard Kentwell

MASTERS PRESS

A Division of Howard W. Sams & Co.

Published by Masters Press
A Division of Howard W. Sams & Company,
2647 Waterfront Pkwy E. Dr, Suite 100, Indianapolis, IN 46214

Printed in the United States of America.

97 98 99 00 01   10 9 8 7 6 5 4 3

Library of Congress Cataloging-in-Publication Data
Dutch soccer drills / Richard Kentwell.
        p.   cm.
      Contents: v. 1. Individual skills
      ISBN 1-57028-106-8 (v. 1)
      1. Soccer--Training.   I. Kentwell, Richard G. R., 1947-
GV943.9.T7D88 1996   96-41894
796.334--dc20   CIP

INTRODUCTION

Dutch Soccer Drills is an aid to creating carefully balanced coaching sessions. The various small sided games and drills are indexed by subject to make it easy to find the drills you need. The value of *Dutch Soccer Drills* is instantly recognizable. How many times has the following scenario happened to you?

> Tonight I have another coaching session. I have no idea which drills I will use. After the last match, the team's shortcomings were fairly obvious. Although we won, we missed far too many goal-scoring opportunities early in the match. We lost the ball too often in midfield, and if the opposition had been sharper we would have conceded a few goals. Something was definitely wrong. Maybe I need to vary the coaching drills I have been using recently. Introduce more obstacles. Gear the exercises more closely to the match situations. Differentiate more. Which players are lacking in self-confidence? Which players still have conditional shortcomings? What should I concentrate on specifically in the coming weeks in the context of our scheduled opponents? And on top of all of that, I need drills which can motivate and capture my players' imagination.

Lots of question for which there are lots of possible answers.

While the match itself offers endless opportunities for creating coaching drills, it is still imperative to have a book containing match-related, small sided games and coaching drills. When planning a coaching program it is important to select the most appropriate drills. *Dutch Soccer Drills* is an excellent aid for devising such a program. A match analysis should be carried out beforehand. This soccer book is an ideal tool to use in conjunction with an in-depth match analysis.

A coach sees a great deal during a match. We usually look first to see whether players are carrying out the tasks they have been assigned. Obviously we are also interested in the result. The impressions gathered during a match are lost after a few hours and certainly after a few days have passed. We can then no longer recall the consecutive phases of the game. If we won, everything must have gone well. If we lost, we look for the moments in the game which were crucial to losing it. In both cases we are taking a one-sided approach to the match. It would be better to make notes on the positive and negative aspects of each match, with a view to remembering strengths and improving weaknesses. The point of departure is always the player. His technical development and tactical insight determine which drills are best for him. Each page shows a diagram with the correct sequence of moves. It also shows the objective of the drill, guidelines relating to the organization, instructions which can be given during the drill, and a number of possible variations. When a coach devises a coaching program, it is essential that enough attention is paid to each type of drill. The focus should not be on the result of the next match but on developing players with good technical skills and tactical insight, and the ability to solve the problems with which they are confronted during games of soccer.

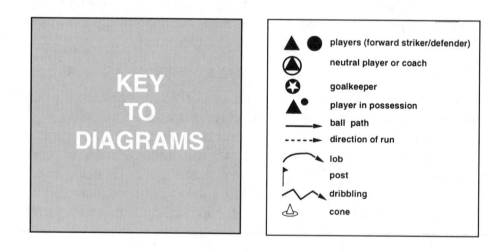

KEY
TO
DIAGRAMS

▲ ●	players (forward striker/defender)
◉	neutral player or coach
✪	goalkeeper
▲•	player in possession
——►	ball path
- - - ►	direction of run
⌒	lob
⌐	post
∧∧	dribbling
△	cone

STEPS FOR USING *DUTCH SOCCER DRILLS*

1. Analysis

• What are the strong and weak points of the team?

• Which phase of training are we in?

• How have we tried to improve weak points until now?

2. Objectives — choice of subject

• What can we achieve in a single coaching session?

• Which subject is important in the context of developments to date or with regard to the next opponent?

3. Planning the coaching session

• Which methodical aspects should be taken into account?

• How should I dose the workload?

• Which small sided games and practice drills should I choose?

4. Giving the coaching session

• Should specific exercises be carried out longer or more intensively?

• Has the desired effect been achieved?

• Do the corrections and instructions bring the desired results?

5. Evaluation of the coaching session

• Did everything go to plan?

• Were the players motivated?

• Did the players learn anything?

Chapter 1

DRIBBLING

DRIBBLING 1

OBJECTIVE:	Learning to dribble in tight spaces
NUMBER OF PLAYERS:	10 - 18
AREA/FIELD:	10 yards x 25 yards
TIME:	5 - 10 minutes
EQUIPMENT:	4 cones, 10 flags, 10 - 18 balls

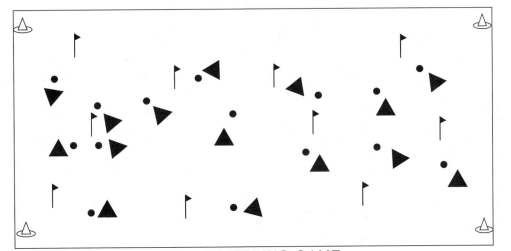

DRIBBLING GAME

ORGANIZATION:	• Players can dribble around freely. • When whistle blows, players must reach a free flag as quickly as possible.
INSTRUCTIONS:	• Tell players to use whole area/field. • Only one player per flag.
COACHING POINTS:	• Keep eyes on field. Watch own ball as little as possible. • Keep ball close to you at all times.
VARIATIONS:	• Reduce number of flags. • Competitive game; who is the first to get 3 points (3 points can be won by getting to a flag 3 consecutive times without missing a turn).

DRIBBLING

OBJECTIVE: Learning to dribble under pressure
Learning to accelerate with ball

NUMBER OF PLAYERS: 16 (4 per grid)

AREA/FIELD: 5 yard grids
15 yard spacing between grids

TIME: 10 minutes

EQUIPMENT: 16 cones, 16 balls

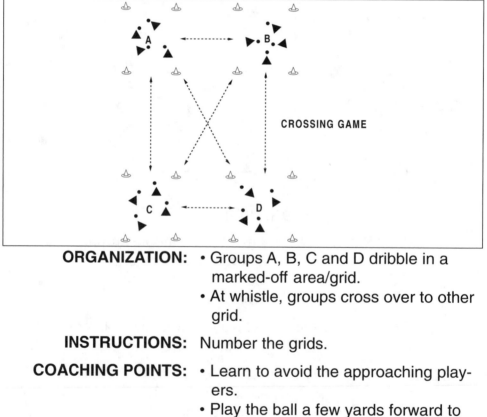

CROSSING GAME

ORGANIZATION: • Groups A, B, C and D dribble in a marked-off area/grid.
• At whistle, groups cross over to other grid.

INSTRUCTIONS: Number the grids.

COACHING POINTS: • Learn to avoid the approaching players.
• Play the ball a few yards forward to go faster (running with ball).
• Control ball in close quarters.
• Control ball at speed while changing grids.

VARIATIONS: Diagonal box interchange.

DRIBBLING

OBJECTIVE: Learning to dribble in tight spaces
Learning to react quickly to a teammate

NUMBER OF PLAYERS: 6 - 10

AREA/FIELD: Grid 20 yards x 20 yards

TIME: 5 minutes

EQUIPMENT: 6 - 10 balls, 4 cones

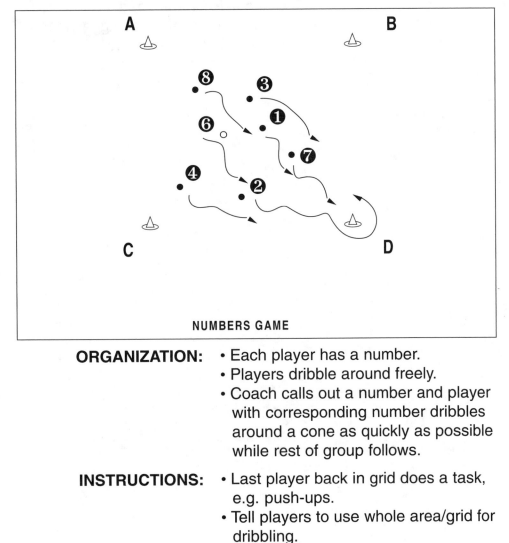

NUMBERS GAME

ORGANIZATION:
- Each player has a number.
- Players dribble around freely.
- Coach calls out a number and player with corresponding number dribbles around a cone as quickly as possible while rest of group follows.

INSTRUCTIONS:
- Last player back in grid does a task, e.g. push-ups.
- Tell players to use whole area/grid for dribbling.

DRIBBLING 3

COACHING POINTS:
- Make fast change of directions by cutting ball.
- Accelerate with ball after command.

VARIATIONS:
- Emphasize stamina by decreasing the length of the recuperation breaks.
- Call out 2 numbers; follow leaders in even groups.
- Call out 1 number; leader goes around one cone, group goes to the diagonally opposite cone.

DRIBBLING 4

OBJECTIVE:	• Learning to dribble and turn with ball by cutting the ball back • Learning to pass
NUMBER OF PLAYERS:	10 - 15
TIME:	5 minutes at each station
EQUIPMENT:	11 cones, 10 - 15 balls

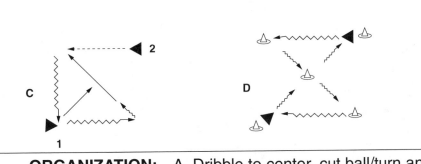

ORGANIZATION: A. Dribble to center, cut ball/turn and dribble back.

B. Player 1 plays ball to player 2. Player 2 dribbles back to player 1, beats player 1 by using fake/feint and passes the ball to player B. Player 3 takes ball, repeat.

C. Dribble to a free corner, cut ball/turn and play ball to player 2 in diagonal corner.

D. Dribble toward center of grid, cut ball/turn and go to next cone (triangle).

DRIBBLING 4

INSTRUCTIONS: All players need to start at same time (stations A, C, D).

COACHING POINTS:
- Dribble with speed.
- Turn/cut ball in various ways.
- Accelerate after turn.

DRIBBLING 5

OBJECTIVE:	Learning to dribble with speed/pace
NUMBER OF PLAYERS:	12
AREA/FIELD:	25 yard dribbling course
TIME:	10 minutes
EQUIPMENT:	13 cones, 4 balls

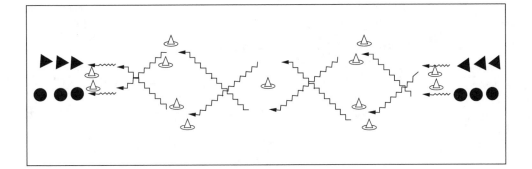

ORGANIZATION:	• Players form 2 competitive groups. • Players compete in 1 v 1 dribbling course.
INSTRUCTIONS:	• Players dribble zig-zag through course. • First player to cross finish line wins game.
COACHING POINTS:	• Keep opponent in view while crossing over. • Keep ball close to feet while changing direction.
VARIATIONS:	• Start with turn. • Let players go through course back and back to the start. • Finish with pass or shot on target.

DRIBBLING

OBJECTIVE: • Learning to dribble and pass
• Improving speed and stamina

NUMBER OF PLAYERS: 12 - 16

AREA/FIELD: Length of field

TIME: 10 - 15 minutes

EQUIPMENT: 12 flags, 8 cones, 2 balls

RELAY

ORGANIZATION: Set up 2 stations. Split up team in 4 groups. Player A starts with pass through flags and sprints around cone. Collect ball and repeat. Having collected the second pass, pass the ball to player B who takes over.

INSTRUCTIONS: Don't make targets too small.

COACHING POINTS: • Concentrate on pass (right direction and pace).
• Collect ball after pass facing next target. Do everything at speed.

VARIATIONS: • Competitive game.
• Vary distance between flags and cones.
• Make smaller targets.

DRIBBLING 7

OBJECTIVE: Learning to dribble, turn and pass

NUMBER OF PLAYERS: 8 - 12

AREA/FIELD: Circle (center circle)

TIME: 10 minutes

EQUIPMENT: 4 balls

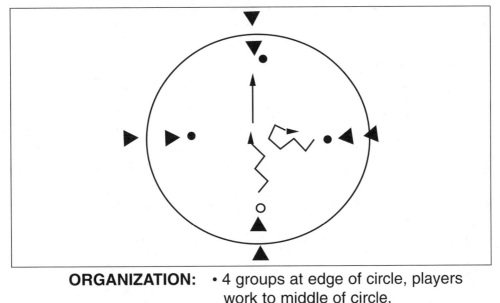

ORGANIZATION:
- 4 groups at edge of circle, players work to middle of circle.
- Players dribble to middle, turn and pass to teammate.

INSTRUCTIONS: Let players start at same time.

COACHING POINTS:
- Practice both feet.
- Dribble and turn at speed.
- Keep control of ball under pressure of approaching players.
- Make ccurate passes.

VARIATIONS: Turn to left/right, pass ball to player on left/right and follow ball after turn, play wallpass with player on edge of circle.

DRIBBLING

OBJECTIVE:	Learning to turn and cut ball using inside and outside of foot
NUMBER OF PLAYERS:	4 per grid
AREA/FIELD:	12 yard x 12 yard grid
TIME:	15 minutes
EQUIPMENT:	4 cones, 2 balls

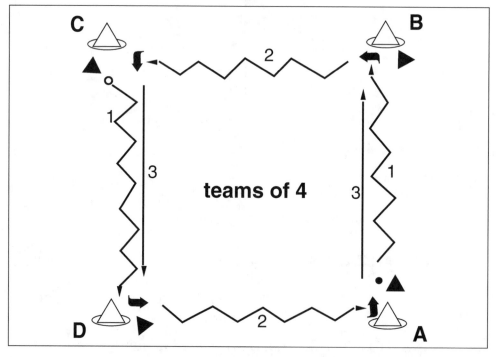

ORGANIZATION:	Player at each corner, players A and C with ball. Players A and C dribble toward B and D, turn/cut ball and dribble to next corner. In corner, pass ball to B and D.
INSTRUCTIONS:	Players start dribbling at same time.
COACHING POINTS:	Use different turns and cuts (step-over, inside/outside, etc).

DRIBBLING 9

OBJECTIVE: • Learning to take on defenders 1 v 1
• Learning to defend a zone

NUMBER OF PLAYERS: 5

AREA/FIELD: 3 grids of 10 yards x 10 yards

TIME: 10 - 15 minutes

EQUIPMENT: 8 cones, 2 balls

ORGANIZATION: • Player A takes on defender B (defending middle grid).
• After beating B, player C defends A. If player A loses ball he becomes a defender. Player D takes on defender B after A has won 1 v 1.

INSTRUCTIONS: Change defenders if they keep losing 1 v 1.

COACHING POINTS: • Take on defenders with speed.
• Accelerate after beating defender.
• Look for second defender quickly.

DRIBBLING 10

OBJECTIVE: Learning to win 2 v 2 (with help of teammate)

NUMBER OF PLAYERS: 8 - 12

AREA/FIELD: 10 yards x 25 yards

TIME: 15 minutes

EQUIPMENT: 8 cones, 1 ball

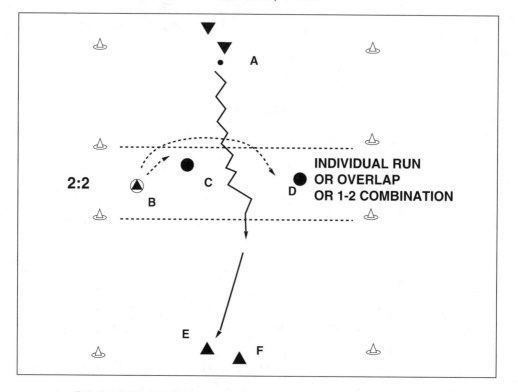

ORGANIZATION:
- Player A dribbles toward 2 defenders (C and D) in middle grid and tries to beat defenders with help of teammate B.
- After beating defenders, A plays ball to player E. Player E repeats drill.

INSTRUCTIONS: Change defenders after they win ball.

DRIBBLING 10

COACHING POINTS:

- Maintaint eyecontact and communication between A and B.
- Use different options to beat defenders;
  - Individual run by A
  - Overlap by B
  - 1-2 combination

VARIATIONS:

- Change defenders after attackers have won five 2 v 2's.
- Defenders can score on a goal after winning ball.

DRIBBLING

OBJECTIVE:	Learning to turn and cut with back to defender
NUMBER OF PLAYERS:	8
AREA/FIELD:	15 yards x 10 yards
TIME:	10 minutes
EQUIPMENT:	3 cones, 2 balls

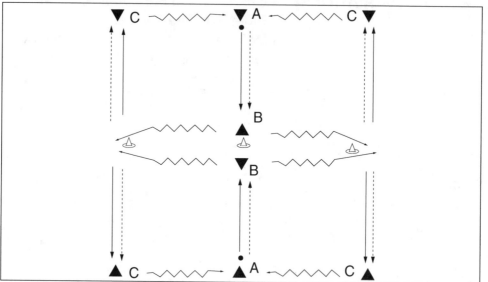

ORGANIZATION: Player A plays ball to B. Player B turns and, with back to cone (hypothetical defender) cuts ball away from cone. After turn/cut, B dribbles past cone and passes to C. Player C dribbles to starting position.

COACHING POINTS:
- Pass ball with pace (from A to B).
- Make quick turns.
- Keep control over ball while turning/ shield ball.
- Accelerate after turn away from cone.

VARIATIONS: Replace cone with defender.

DRIBBLING 12

OBJECTIVE:	Learning to penetrate/dribble into oppositions' half by turning/cutting with ball
NUMBER OF PLAYERS:	4
AREA/FIELD:	10 yards x 20 yards
TIME:	10 minutes
EQUIPMENT:	4 cones or flags, 2 balls

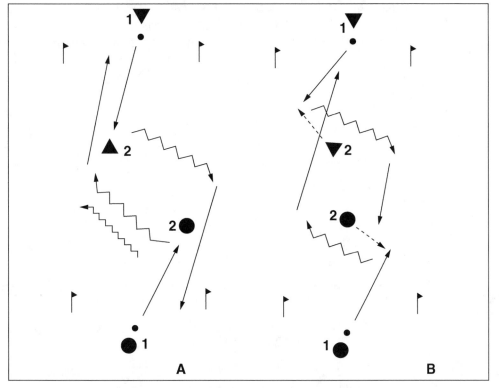

ORGANIZATION:	Player 1 passes to player 2. Player 2 turns quickly to his right while cutting ball. After turn, accelerates and dribbles with ball. Player 2 passes to player 1 on other side.
INSTRUCTIONS:	Let both sides start at same time to avoid collision.

DRIBBLING 12

COACHING POINTS:
- Communication between players 1 and 2.
- Player 2 cut ball with inside left or outside right foot.
- While cutting/turning keep ball close to feet.
- Use body fake to opposite direction before cutting.

VARIATIONS:
- Add defenders for more pressure.
- **Diagram B:** Player makes run before receiving ball and turning with it.

DRIBBLING   13

OBJECTIVE: Dribbling combined with passing (long pass, wallpass, and shooting)

NUMBER OF PLAYERS: 6

AREA/FIELD: 25 yards x 25 yards

TIME: 15 minutes

EQUIPMENT: 6 cones, 2 balls

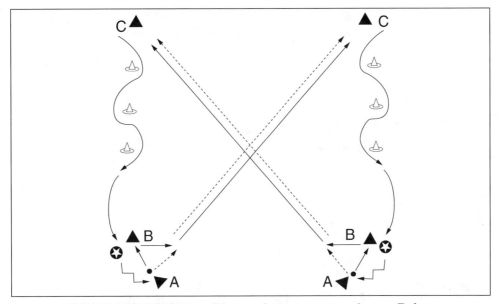

ORGANIZATION: Player A passes to player B for wallpass. Player A controls ball and plays long pass to player C. Player C receives ball and dribbles through cones. After last cone, C shoots on goalkeeper who saves and throws ball to player A.

COACHING POINTS:
- Make hard, direct passes.
- Pass from player B into player A's run.

VARIATIONS:
- Only high or ground balls to player C.
- Everything one touch.
- Shot on goal after dribble through cones.

DRIBBLING

OBJECTIVE:	Beating a defender on the dribble (defender defending a line)
NUMBER OF PLAYERS:	8 - 12
AREA/FIELD:	Grids 10 yards x 10 yards
TIME:	10 - 15 minutes
EQUIPMENT:	8 cones, 2 balls

ORGANIZATION:	Defenders A and B both defend line in middle of grid. Attackers try to go over line by beating defenders. After beating defenders, pass to player at end of grid.
INSTRUCTIONS:	Defenders change after they win ball.
COACHING POINTS:	• Go at defenders with speed. • Fake/faint on time. • Pass ball after beating defender.
VARIATIONS:	• Decrease width of field. • After beating defender, score on small goal by pass.

DRILLING

DRIBBLING 15

OBJECTIVE: Learning to beat a defender
Learning to win the ball

NUMBER OF PLAYERS: 8 - 16

AREA/FIELD: 10 yard x 10 yard grids

TIME: 15 - 20 minutes

EQUIPMENT: 1 ball per grid, 6 cones

no interception   interception

C   C

B   B

A   A

ORGANIZATION:
• Player A takes on defender B. After beating defender he passes ball to player on opposite side of grid.
• Player C becomes defender and player B takes player A's position.

INSTRUCTIONS: If defender B intercepts ball he passes ball to player on side of grid, who takes on player C.

COACHING POINTS:
• Take on defender with speed.
• After beating defender, pass to team-mate quickly and accurately.
• When defender wins ball, make quick transitions from offense/defense.

VARIATIONS: Decrease width of field.

DRIBBLING

OBJECTIVE: Improving passing and taking on defenders

NUMBER OF PLAYERS: 4 per station

AREA/FIELD: 10 yard x 40 yard grids

TIME: 20 minutes

EQUIPMENT: 20 cones, 4 balls

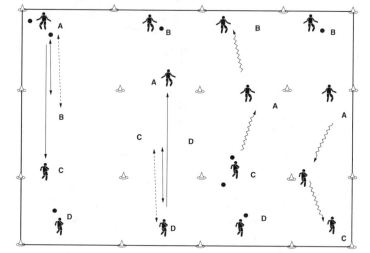

ORGANIZATION:
- Station 1: Player A passes to player B, wallpass by player B. Player A passes to player C, who receives, turns and plays a wallpass with D.
- Station 2: Player C goes 1 v 1 with player A. After beating player A, 1 v 1 with player B.

INSTRUCTIONS: Players rotate as follows; A becomes D, B - A, C - B, D - C.

COACHING POINTS:
- Before passing, players must have eye contact.
- Use proper technique and surface of foot for passing.

VARIATIONS: Use 1 touch in passing drill.

DRIBBLING   17

OBJECTIVE: Dribbling, shielding and wallpassing under pressure of defender

NUMBER OF PLAYERS: 16 (4 groups of 4)

AREA/FIELD: 2 grids of 15 yards x 15 yards

TIME: 12 - 20 minutes

EQUIPMENT: 6 cones, 4 balls

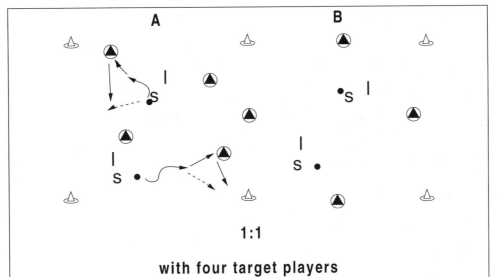

1:1

with four target players

ORGANIZATION:
- Two players with ball each, 2 defenders and 4 neutral players per grid.
- Two players with ball dribble inside grid. Defenders try to win ball. Players with ball can use neutral players as teammates.

INSTRUCTIONS: Switch players after 1 minute.

COACHING POINTS:
- Play with head up, look at neutral players for passing options.
- Shield ball when no options (dribble, pass) are available.
- Keep moving with ball.

DRIBBLING 17

VARIATIONS: • Neutral players can move around freely inside grid.
• Neutral players must be stationary on perimeter of grid.
• Restrictions for neutral players such as 1 touch.

DRIBBLING 18

OBJECTIVE:	Learning to play 1 v 1, offense and defense
NUMBER OF PLAYERS:	10 - 16
AREA/FIELD:	30 yards x 30 yards
TIME:	10 minutes
EQUIPMENT:	5 - 8 goals, supply of balls

ORGANIZATION:	• Pairs of players play 1 v 1 inside field. • Players can score by dribbling through cones.
INSTRUCTIONS:	• If defender wins ball, he becomes offensive player.
COACHING POINTS:	• Change direction and speed with ball. • Use whole field. • Look up to see field and open goals.
VARIATIONS:	• Score by passing through goal. • One player plays offense for set time; how many goals can he score in set time.

DRIBBLING 19

OBJECTIVE: Practicing faking/feinting while taking on defender

NUMBER OF PLAYERS: 8 - 12

AREA/FIELD: Half field

TIME: 25 minutes

EQUIPMENT: 3 cones, goal, supply of balls

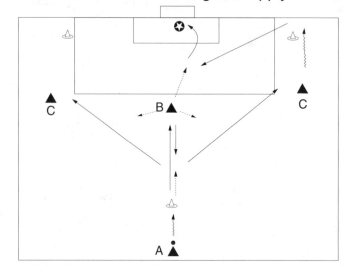

ORGANIZATION: Player A dribbles toward cone, fake to right or left then passes to player B. Player B passes back to player A who passes to player C on flank. Player C dribbles toward cone, fakes and crosses to player B in front of goal. Player B shoots on goal.

COACHING POINTS:
- Dribble, pass and cross at game speed.
- Fake to left and right side.
- Make eye contact when passing.

VARIATIONS:
- All passing 1 touch.
- Both player A and B make run to goal for finish.

Chapter 2

PASSING

PASSING

OBJECTIVE: Learning to pass and place ball in various directions under pressure

NUMBER OF PLAYERS: 12

AREA/FIELD: Half field

TIME: 15 minutes

EQUIPMENT: A: 2 balls per 3 players
B: 1 ball per 3 players

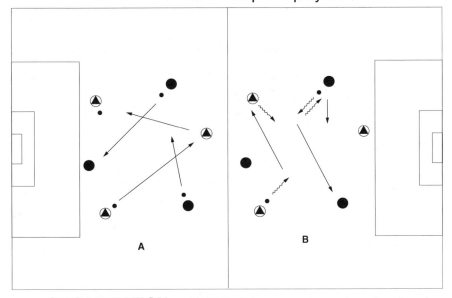

ORGANIZATION: Drill A: Players are set up in circular formation. Players with ball look for open players to pass to. After pass, be ready to receive next pass.
Drill B: Players with ball dribble to middle and pass to open player. If nobody is open, dribble back and then look for pass.

INSTRUCTIONS: Make sure all players are involved and ready to pass and receive.

COACHING POINTS: Passer and receiver make eye contact.

PASSING 1

Make accurate passes.
Communicate.

VARIATIONS: • Drill A: Play 1 touch.
• Let players move around freely inside half of field.

PASSING 2

OBJECTIVE:	Learning to pass over longer distance
NUMBER OF PLAYERS:	6 - 8 (3 or 4 per grid)
AREA/FIELD:	2 grids of 10 yards x 20 yards Distance between grids; 20 yards
TIME:	10 minutes
EQUIPMENT:	8 cones, 1 ball

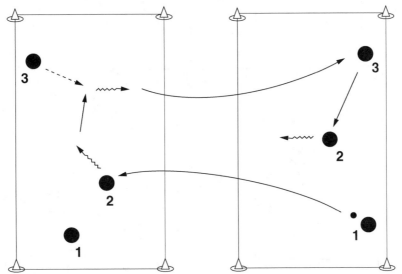

ORGANIZATION:
- Player 1 passes ball to player 2 in other grid.
- Player 2 receives, dribbles and passes ball to player 3. Player 3 plays long ball to other grid.

INSTRUCTIONS: Keep all players moving, with or without ball.

COACHING POINTS:
- Communicate before passing.
- Play ball to moving player (run into space).

VARIATIONS:
- Play 1 touch.
- Vary distance between grids.
- Use 2 balls at same time.

PASSING

OBJECTIVE: Learning to pass on the move

NUMBER OF PLAYERS: 10

AREA/FIELD: 25 yards x 25 yards

TIME: 10 - 15 minutes

EQUIPMENT: 1 ball

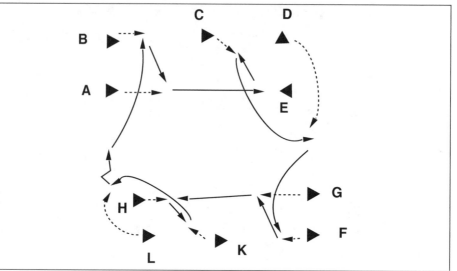

ORGANIZATION: Player A passes to player E, one-touch pass to player C who passes long to moving player D. Player D passes to moving player F. Player F wall passes to player G. Drill repeats with players K, H, L and B.

INSTRUCTIONS:
- Keep square shape for drill.
- Players change directions after pass and run except D, E, H and L.

COACHING POINTS:
- Communicate and make eye contact.
- Use inside foot for wallpass.
- Pass accurately with good pace.
- Time the runs.

VARIATIONS: Use 2 balls simultaneously.

PASSING 4

OBJECTIVE: Learning to pass, move and play 1-2 combination

NUMBER OF PLAYERS: Groups of 3 plus neutral players

AREA/FIELD: Half field

TIME: 10 minutes

EQUIPMENT: 1 ball per 3 players

ORGANIZATION: Groups of 3 move around freely. Players have 3 options:
1. Players 1 and 2 play 1-2 combination before passing to 3.
2. Player 1 dribbles the ball, player 2 makes a run away from ball before checking back to ball. Player 2 receives ball, turns and repeats drill.
3. Use extra player for 1-2 combination before passing to teammate.

COACHING POINTS:
• Play 1 touch whenever possible.
• Play ball alternately low and high.
• Vary distance between players.

VARIATIONS: Introduce defenders.

PASSING 5

OBJECTIVE:
- Reading the flight of the ball
- Supporting the player with the ball by making a run

NUMBER OF PLAYERS: Groups of 4

AREA/FIELD: 30 yards x 15 yards

TIME: 10 minutes

EQUIPMENT: 3 cones, 1 ball

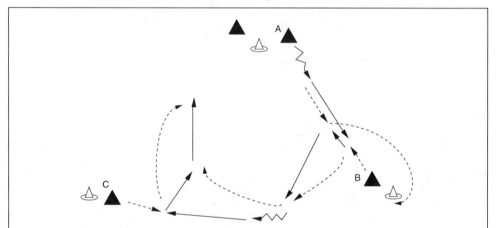

ORGANIZATION:
- Player A dribbles towards player B.
- Player B shows for ball, wallpass back to player A.
- Player A passes ball into run of player B.
- Player B collects ball and repeats with player C.

INSTRUCTIONS: Let players execute at game speed.

COACHING POINTS:
- Ask for ball at right moment.
- Put correct pace on the ball.
- Keep correct distance between players.
- Communicate and make eye contact.

VARIATIONS: Introduce defender behind receiving player.

PASSING 6

OBJECTIVE:	Reading the flight of the ball
NUMBER OF PLAYERS:	Groups of 3
AREA/FIELD:	30 yards x 15 yards
TIME:	10 minutes
EQUIPMENT:	3 cones 1 ball

ORGANIZATION:
- Player A passes ball to player B who shows for ball.
- Player A overlaps Player B after pass.
- Player B turns with ball toward player C, who is making a run.
- Player B passes ball into path of player C.

INSTRUCTIONS: Let player execute at game speed.

COACHING POINTS: Keep communication and eye contact with passer.

VARIATIONS: Introduce defender.

PASSING

OBJECTIVE:	Reading the flight of the ball Learning to anticipate
NUMBER OF PLAYERS:	Groups of 4
AREA/FIELD:	30 yards x 30 yards
TIME:	10 minutes
EQUIPMENT:	3 cones, 1 ball

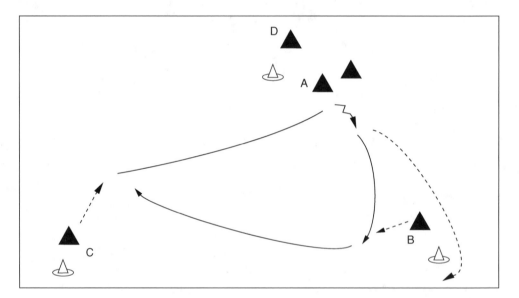

ORGANIZATION:
- Player A gives a high pass off the dribble to player B, who is making a run.
- Player B passes the ball, 1 touch to player C who is making a run.
- Player C controls ball, and plays a high pass to player D.

COACHING POINTS:
- Put correct pace on ball.
- Receive and control ball in the direction of your next move or pass.

VARIATIONS: Introduce defenders.

PASSING 8

OBJECTIVE:	Learning to pass accurately at the right pace
NUMBER OF PLAYERS:	Groups of 3 and 4
AREA/FIELD:	Grid of 10 yards x 30 yards
TIME:	10 minutes
EQUIPMENT:	2 balls for group A, 1 ball for group B

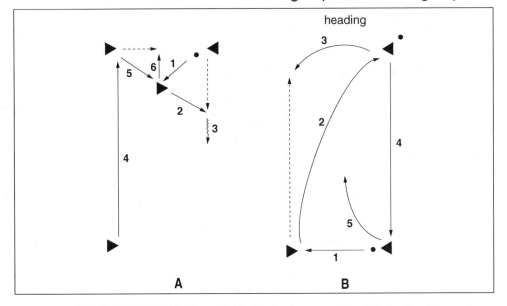

ORGANIZATION:	Drill A: 3 players, 2 with ball plus extra player as lay off player.
	• Player with ball makes a short 1-2 combination with lay off player, then dribbles to free corner.
	• Player 2 gives a long ball to third player, who receives and then makes a short 1-2 combination with lay off player, then dribbles to free corner.
	Drill B: 3 players with ball.
	• Player 1 passes to player 2 who gives a long pass to player 3. Player 3 heads ball to free corner where

PASSING

player 2 is making a run. Player 2 passes to player 1.

COACHING POINTS:
- Play one touch if possible.
- Concentrate on accuracy.

PASSING 9

OBJECTIVE:	Learning to pass and change direction
NUMBER OF PLAYERS:	Groups of 6
AREA/FIELD:	20 yards x 20 yards
TIME:	10 minutes
EQUIPMENT:	3 cones, 1 ball

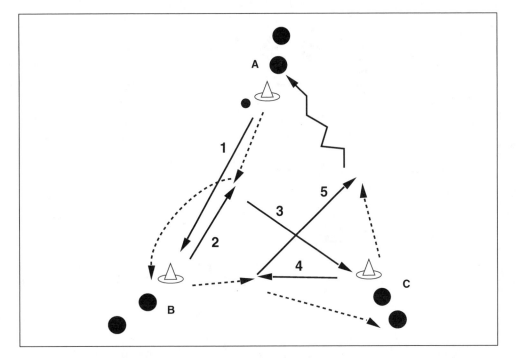

ORGANIZATION:
- Player A passes to player B. Player B wallpasses ball back to A and makes run around cone.
- Player A plays ball to player C who wall passes it to player B after he comes around cone.
- Player B plays ball into run of player C who finishes drill with dribble.

INSTRUCTIONS: Start drill off with 2 or more touches per player.

PASSING 9

COACHING POINTS:
- Communicate, make eye contact.
- Pace the ball.
- Time the runs.

VARIATIONS:
- Low and high balls.
- Heading.
- One touch play.

PASSING 10

OBJECTIVE: Learning to time runs and passes

NUMBER OF PLAYERS: 10

AREA/FIELD: 15 yards x 15 yards

TIME: 15 minutes

EQUIPMENT: 4 cones, 1 ball

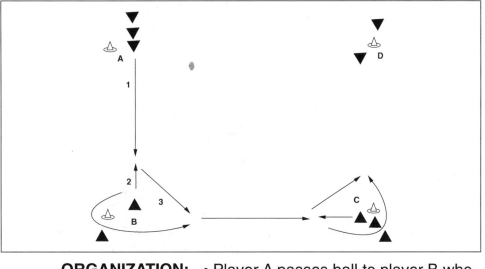

ORGANIZATION:
- Player A passes ball to player B who shows for ball.
- Player B plays ball back to player A and makes a quick run around cone.
- Player A passes ball into player B's run.

COACHING POINTS:
- Concentrate on accurate passing.
- Player B run quick to ball (to show for ball).
- Time run and pass.

VARIATIONS:
- Make grid smaller.
- If the skill is high enough, the drill can be performed with 2 balls simultaneously; players A and C start at the same time.

PASSING

OBJECTIVE: Learning to time runs and passes

NUMBER OF PLAYERS: 10

AREA/FIELD: 15 yards x 15 yards

TIME: 15 minutes

EQUIPMENT: 4 cones, 1 ball

ORGANIZATION: Player A passes ball to player B, who shows for ball. Player B plays ball back to player A and makes run around cone. Player A passes ball to player C. Player C plays ball to player B. Player B passes ball to player D. Player C makes run around cone and shows for ball from player D. Finish with diagonal pass to A.

COACHING POINTS:
- Concentrate on accurate passing.
- Time runs and passes.
- Communicate.
- Make quick runs to ball and around cones (Fast footwork).

VARIATIONS:
- Make grid smaller.
- Play 1 touch.
- Use 2 balls simultaneously.
- Players A and C start at same time.

PASSING 12

OBJECTIVE: Learning to show for ball and passing under pressure

NUMBER OF PLAYERS: 8

AREA/FIELD: 25 yards x 25 yards

TIME: 10 minutes

EQUIPMENT: 4 cones 2 balls

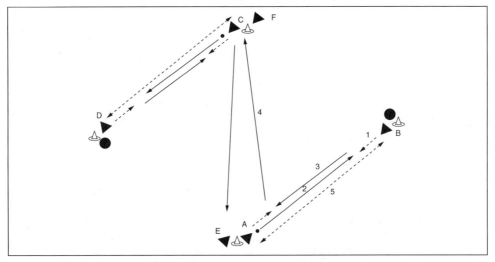

ORGANIZATION:
- Players A and C pass to B and D respectively.
- Players B and D pass back. Players A and C play a diagonal ball to players F and E respectively.
- Players B and D are pressured from behind by defenders.

INSTRUCTIONS:
- Let players switch postions.
- Let defenders defend at 50% at start of drill.
- Let A and C start at same time.

COACHING POINTS:
- Hold off/shield defenders while making wallpass.
- Concentrate on accurate passing.

PASSING 12

- Use left and right foot.
- Make diagonal pass through air.

VARIATIONS: Use defenders on all players.

OBJECTIVE:	Learning to pass after cutting ball
NUMBER OF PLAYERS:	Groups of 4
AREA/FIELD:	20 yards x 20 yards
TIME:	10 minutes
EQUIPMENT:	4 cones 2 balls

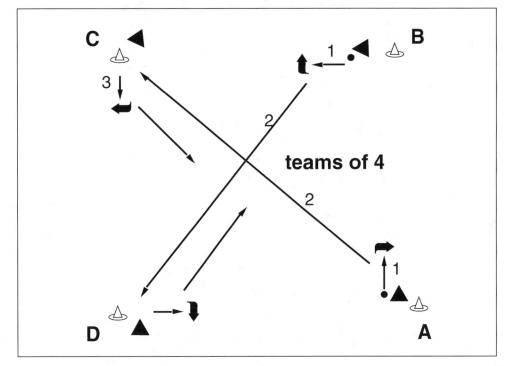

ORGANIZATION:	Players A and C start dribbling, after 1 or 2 yards cut ball and play a diagonal ball to C and D respectively.
INSTRUCTIONS:	Let players use different cuts and turns.
COACHING POINTS:	• Keep ball close to feet on dribble and after cut/turn. • Know where teammate is for quick, accurate passing.
VARIATIONS:	Either high or low passes.

PASSING

OBJECTIVE:	Learning to wallpass in a 1-3 combination
NUMBER OF PLAYERS:	Groups of 6
AREA/FIELD:	15 yards x 15 yards
TIME:	10 - 15 minutes
EQUIPMENT:	4 cones, 1 ball

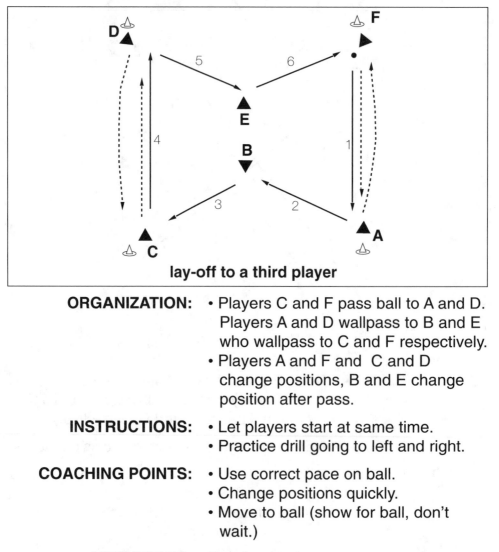

lay-off to a third player

ORGANIZATION:	• Players C and F pass ball to A and D. Players A and D wallpass to B and E who wallpass to C and F respectively.
	• Players A and F and C and D change positions, B and E change position after pass.
INSTRUCTIONS:	• Let players start at same time.
	• Practice drill going to left and right.
COACHING POINTS:	• Use correct pace on ball.
	• Change positions quickly.
	• Move to ball (show for ball, don't wait.)
VARIATIONS:	Passing in air.

PASSING 15

OBJECTIVE: Learning to wallpass and make overlapping runs

NUMBER OF PLAYERS: Groups of 5

AREA/FIELD: 20 yards x 20 yards

TIME: 10 minutes

EQUIPMENT: 3 cones, 1 ball

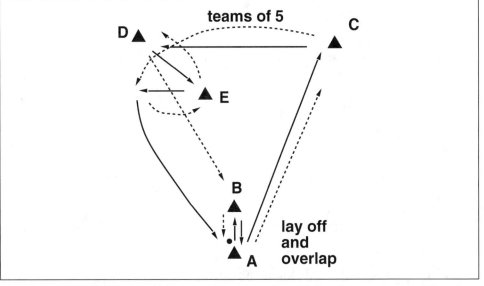

ORGANIZATION • Players A and B play 1-2 combination (wallpass).
• Player A plays long ball to player C and makes run to player C position. Player C plays ball to player D. Player D plays short ball to E and follows pass. Player E lays off ball to overlapping player C who plays long ball to B.

COACHING POINTS: • Make quick overlapping runs.
• Move to ball (show for ball).
• execute accurate passes.
• Communicate, call for ball on run.

PASSING 16

OBJECTIVE:	Learning to pass
NUMBER OF PLAYERS:	7 - 10
AREA/FIELD:	15 yards x 15 yards
TIME:	15 - 20 minutes
EQUIPMENT:	5 cones, 1 ball

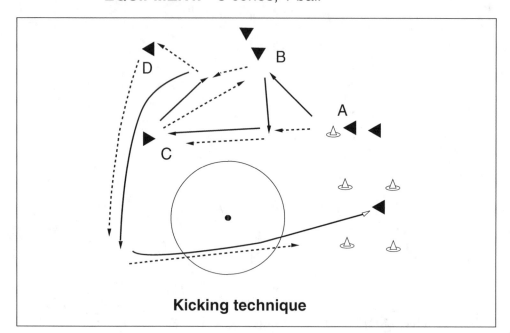

Kicking technique

ORGANIZATION: Players A and B play 1-2 combination. Player A plays ball to player C who plays ball to player B. Player B plays long pass to overlapping player D. Player D receives ball and passes ball into marked off area.

COACHING POINTS: • Show for ball.
• Follow pass.
• Concentrate on accurate passing.

VARIATIONS: • Play 1 touch.
• Final pass is shot on goal.

OBJECTIVE: Learning to cross after beating defenders

NUMBER OF PLAYERS: 8 - 14

AREA/FIELD: 30 yards x 45 yards

TIME: 15 - 20 minutes

EQUIPMENT: 4 flags, 2 goals, 10 balls

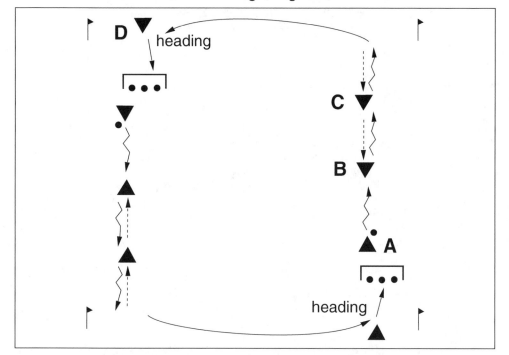

ORGANIZATION: Player A takes on defenders B and C. After beating defenders he crosses ball to player D who finishes on goal.

INSTRUCTIONS:
- 2 groups work at same time.
- Use goalkeepers.

COACHING POINTS:
- Take on defenders with speed.
- After beating last defender make quick, accurate cross.
- Choose right moment and time run to finish cross.

PASSING 18

OBJECTIVE: Learning to pass, lay off ball (wallpass) and cross ball

NUMBER OF PLAYERS: 8 - 14

AREA/FIELD: 30 yards x 45 yards

TIME: 15 - 20 minutes

EQUIPMENT: 4 flags, 2 goals, 10 balls

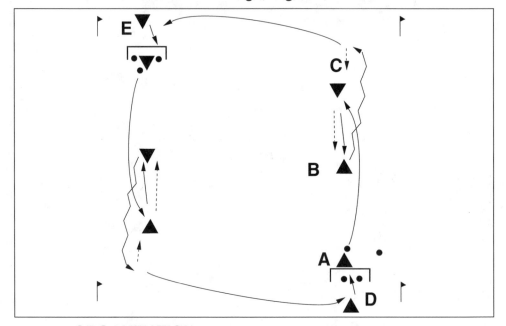

ORGANIZATION: Player A passes ball to player C. Player C lays off ball to player B. B receives ball and takes on player C. After beating C, crosses to player E who finishes at goal.

INSTRUCTIONS:
- Let players start at same time.
- Change positions.

COACHING POINTS:
- Concentrate on accurate passing (long and short).
- Time run to meet cross.
- Run into cross (start at far post).

PASSING   19

OBJECTIVE:	Learning to cross and finish from cross
NUMBER OF PLAYERS:	2 groups of 3
AREA/FIELD:	30 yards x 45 yards
TIME:	15 - 20 minutes
EQUIPMENT:	4 flags, 2 goals, 10 balls

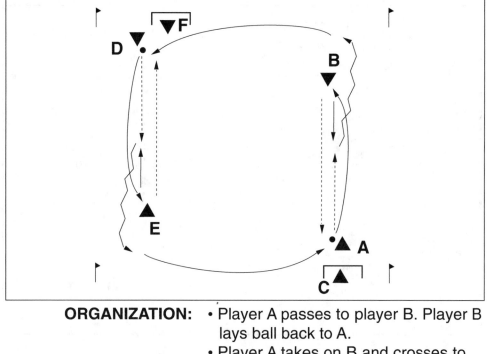

ORGANIZATION:
- Player A passes to player B. Player B lays ball back to A.
- Player A takes on B and crosses to player E.
- Player B moves to finish cross from other group.

INSTRUCTIONS:
- 2 groups work simultaneously.
- Low pressure from defenders to make drill work.

COACHING POINTS:
- Execute drill at high speed.
- Make eye contact before cross.

VARIATIONS: Use goalkeepers.

PASSING   20

OBJECTIVE:	Learning to pass, lay off and cross ball
NUMBER OF PLAYERS:	2 groups of 3
AREA/FIELD:	30 yards x 45 yards
TIME:	15 - 20 minutes
EQUIPMENT:	4 flags, 2 goals, 10 balls

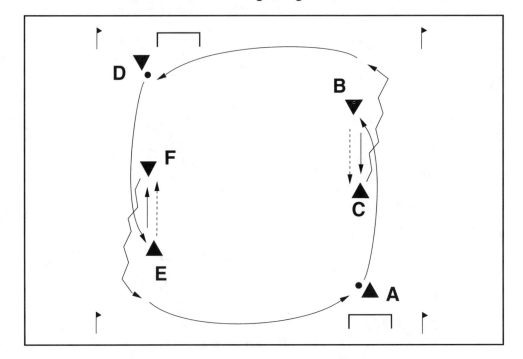

ORGANIZATION:	• Player A passes(chip) to player B. Player B lays off to player C. • Player C takes on B and crosses to player D who finishes on goal.
INSTRUCTIONS:	Low pressure defenders at start of drill.
COACHING POINTS:	• Communicate and make eye contact. • Concentrate on accurate passing.
VARIATIONS:	Use goalkeepers and defenders in front of goal.

PASSING 21

OBJECTIVE: Learning to cross ball after beating defender

NUMBER OF PLAYERS: Groups of 6

AREA/FIELD: 30 yards x 45 yards

TIME: 15 - 20 minutes

EQUIPMENT: 4 flags, 2 goals, 10 balls

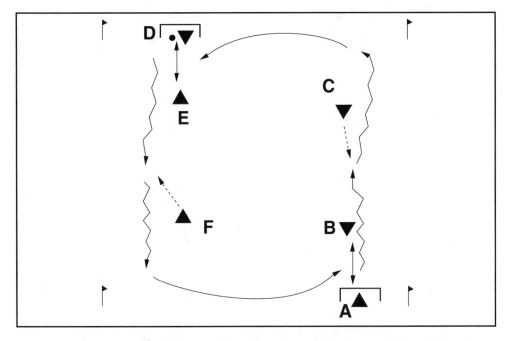

ORGANIZATION: Players A and B play 1-2 combination. After receiving ball back player A takes on player C. After beating C, Cross to player E.

COACHING POINTS: • Maintain communication and eye contact between player crossing ball and player in front of goal.
• Player finishing has to be moving.

VARIATIONS: Use goalkeepers and defenders in front of goal.

OBJECTIVE:	Learning to chip/high pass and cross ball
NUMBER OF PLAYERS:	Groups of 6
AREA/FIELD:	30 yards x 45 yards
TIME:	15 - 20 minutes
EQUIPMENT:	4 flags, 2 goals, supply of balls

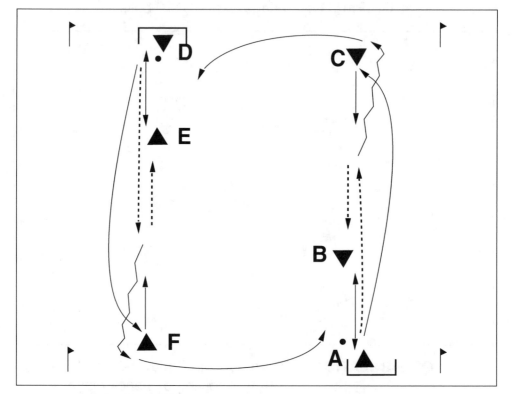

ORGANIZATION: Players A and B play 1-2 combination. Player A chips ball to player C. Player C lays off to player A who dribbles and crosses ball to player E.

COACHING POINTS:
- Player E in front of goal makes an angled run to far post.
- communication and eye contact.

VARIATIONS: Introduce goalkeeper and defenders.

PASSING 23

OBJECTIVE:	Improving passing and turning with ball
NUMBER OF PLAYERS:	10 - 12
AREA/FIELD:	30 yards x 40 yards
TIME:	15 minutes
EQUIPMENT:	5 cones, supply of balls

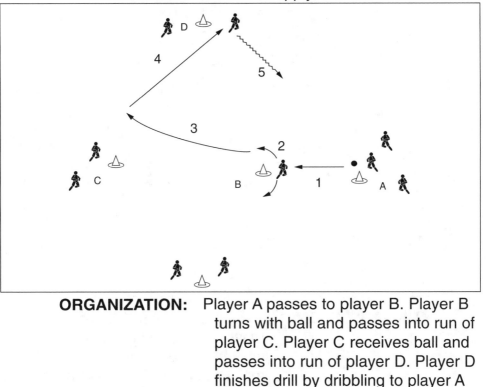

ORGANIZATION:	Player A passes to player B. Player B turns with ball and passes into run of player C. Player C receives ball and passes into run of player D. Player D finishes drill by dribbling to player A position.
INSTRUCTIONS:	Let players in player B position turn left and right.
COACHING POINTS:	• Keep correct pace on ball. • Execute drill at high speed. • Practice correct timing of pass and run.
VARIATIONS:	Introduce defender at position of player B.

OBJECTIVE:	Improving passing and 1-2 combination
NUMBER OF PLAYERS:	10 - 12
AREA/FIELD:	30 yards x 40 yards
TIME:	15 minutes
EQUIPMENT:	5 cones, supply of balls

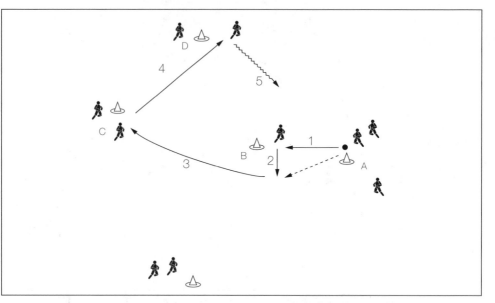

ORGANIZATION:	Player A and B play 1-2 combination. Player A receives ball and passes ball into run of player C. Player C receives ball and passes ball into run of player D. Player D finishes drill by dribbling to player A position.
INSTRUCTIONS:	Let player in B position turn left and right.
COACHING POINTS:	• Keep correct pace on ball. • Execute drill at high speed. • Practice correct timing of run and pass.
VARIATIONS:	Introduce defender at B position.

PASSING 25

OBJECTIVE: Improving passing and 1-2 combination

NUMBER OF PLAYERS: 10 - 12

AREA/FIELD: 10 yards x 30 yards

TIME: 15 minutes

EQUIPMENT: 4 cones, supply of balls

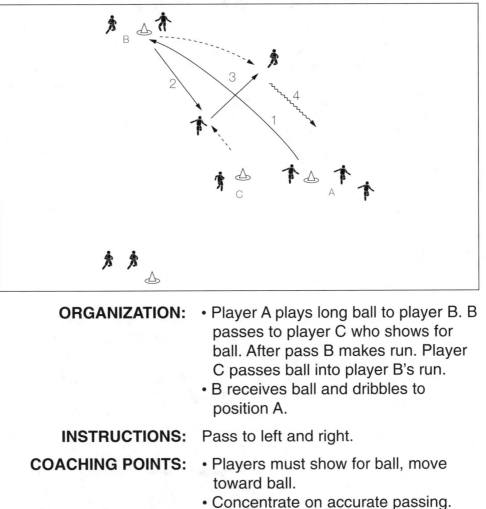

ORGANIZATION:
- Player A plays long ball to player B. B passes to player C who shows for ball. After pass B makes run. Player C passes ball into player B's run.
- B receives ball and dribbles to position A.

INSTRUCTIONS: Pass to left and right.

COACHING POINTS:
- Players must show for ball, move toward ball.
- Concentrate on accurate passing.
- Correct timing of runs.

VARIATIONS: Play one touch.

PASSING 26

OBJECTIVE: Improving passing, movement with and without ball

NUMBER OF PLAYERS: Groups of 2

AREA/FIELD: Let pairs move freely over whole field

TIME: 10 - 15 minutes

EQUIPMENT: 1 ball per 2 players

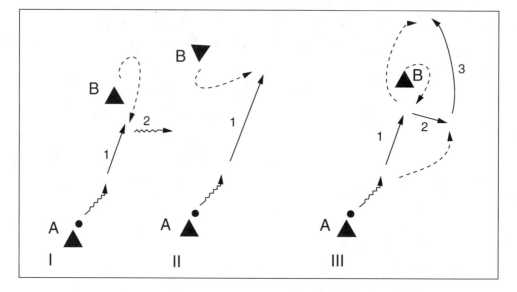

ORGANIZATION:

1. Player A dribbles ball. Player B makes run away from ball then checks back to receive ball and dribble to side.

2. Player A dribbles ball. Player B makes run away from ball into space. Player A passes ball into run of B.

3. Player A dribbles ball. Player B makes run away from ball then checks back and makes 1-2 combination with A. After 1-2 combination player B makes run into space.

PASSING 26

INSTRUCTIONS: Player A passes into run.

COACHING POINTS: Let all groups try all variations.

- Make run away from ball to create time and space (draw away defenders).
- Improve timing of run and pass.
- Communicate and eye contact.
- Play one touch in combinations.

PASSING 27

OBJECTIVE:	Improving passing, 1-2 combination and turning with ball
NUMBER OF PLAYERS:	8 - 12
AREA/FIELD:	20 yards x 20 yards
TIME:	15 minutes
EQUIPMENT:	4 cones, supply of balls

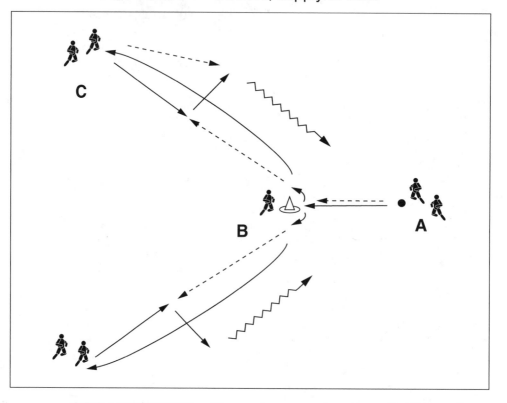

ORGANIZATION:	Player A passes to player B. Player B turns with ball and plays a long 1-2 combination with player C. Player C receives ball and dribbles to position A.
COACHING POINTS:	• Follow pass by sprint/fast run. • Show for ball. • 1-2 combination on ground.

PASSING 28

OBJECTIVE:	Improving passing short and long
NUMBER OF PLAYERS:	Groups of 3
AREA/FIELD:	10 yards x 35 yards
TIME:	10 - 15 minutes
EQUIPMENT:	1 ball per 3 players

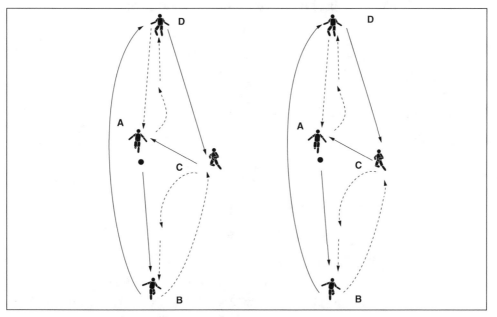

ORGANIZATION: Player A passes ball to player B, who passes a long ball to player D. After pass B makes run to C position. Player D plays 1-2 combination with player B. A runs to position D. Player D makes run to A position after receiving ball. Player D passes to player B who has run back to position B.

COACHING POINTS: • Constantly move and change position.
• Make accurate passes.

VARIATIONS: Play one touch.

PASSING 29

OBJECTIVE: Learning to crosspass in game situations

NUMBER OF PLAYERS: 8

AREA/FIELD: 2 grids of 15 yards x 20 yards
Distance between grids is 30-40 yards

TIME: 15-20 minutes

EQUIPMENT: 1 ball-field marking, e.g. cones

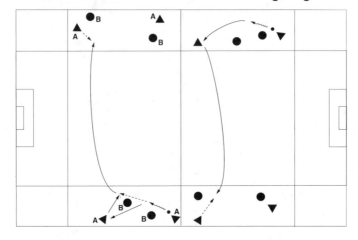

ORGANIZATION:
- 2 v 2 game (team A and B).
- After a player has created time and space in game he plays a crosspass to a teammate in other grid. After receiving ball other team plays 2 v 2.

INSTRUCTIONS: Start game with low pressure defense, to create time and space for crosspass.

COACHING POINTS:
- Wait for right moment to pass.
- Don't force pass.
- Maintain communication between teammates in opposite fields.
- Receiving players keep moving.

VARIATIONS:
- Play 3 v 3, 4 v 4 games.
- Play numbers up, e.g. 4 v 3.

PASSING

OBJECTIVE: Learning to cross and finish under pressure of defender

NUMBER OF PLAYERS: Groups of 4

AREA/FIELD: Half field

TIME: 20 - 25 minutes

EQUIPMENT: 8 cones, goal, supply of balls

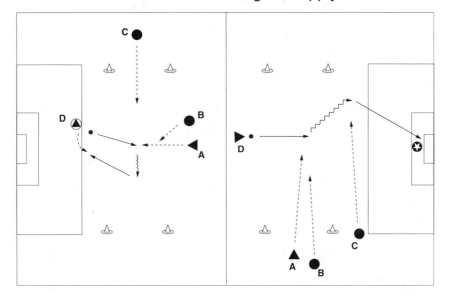

ORGANIZATION: Player D passes ball to player A who is showing for ball. Player A tries to receive, dribble and pass back to D, or shoot at goal, under pressure of B and C.

INSTRUCTIONS: Start with low pressure from defenders.

COACHING POINTS:
- Shield ball while receiving and dribbling.
- Play with head up to see defenders, goalkeeper and teammates.
- Play/dribble at game speed.

VARIATIONS: Player D plays ball to player A in various ways; volley, throw in, etc.

PASSING

OBJECTIVE: Improving passing in various situations

NUMBER OF PLAYERS: Groups of 2

AREA/FIELD: Full field

TIME: 5 minutes per station

EQUIPMENT: Supply of balls, 2 goals

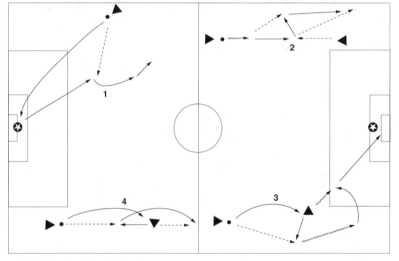

ORGANIZATION:
1. Pass ball back to goalkeeper, move into new space and receive ball back.
2. Dribble, play two wallpasses with cutting teammate.
3. 1-2 combination overlap on flank, pass back to teammate who dribbles toward goal and finishes with shot.
4. Long pass in air, wallpass, long pass in air into partners run.

COACHING POINTS:
• Execute all drills at game speed.
• Make accurate passes (to assure good combinations).

VARIATIONS: Introduce defenders in all drills.

PASSING 32

OBJECTIVE:	Accuracy in passing and shooting
NUMBER OF PLAYERS:	4 per station
AREA/FIELD:	Full field
TIME:	10 minutes per station
EQUIPMENT:	12 cones, 2 goals, 2 boards, supply of balls

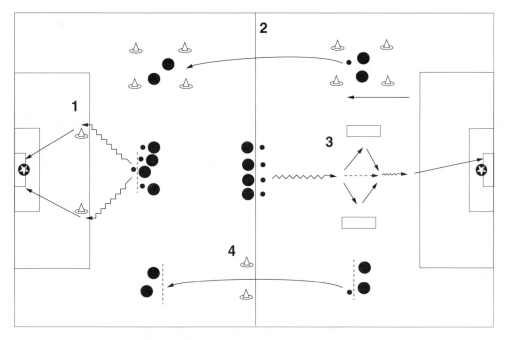

ORGANIZATION:	1. Dribble around cone, shoot at goal.
	2. Accurate passing. Score by passing into opposite grid.
	3. Dribble, pass against board, receive ball and finish on goal.
	4. Low long passing between cones.
INSTRUCTIONS:	Keep score at all stations (competitive game).
COACHING POINTS:	Concentrate on passing and shooting at all stations.

PASSING

OBJECTIVE:	Improving passing and stamina in various stations
NUMBER OF PLAYERS:	4 per station
AREA/FIELD:	Full field
TIME:	10 - 15 minutes per station
EQUIPMENT:	2 goals, 4 cones, supply of balls

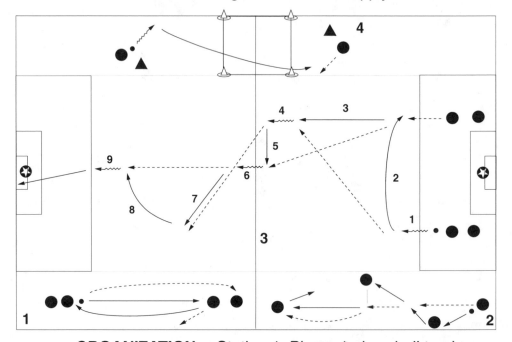

ORGANIZATION: Station 1: Player 1 plays ball to player 2 (30 yards) and follows pass.
Station 2: Player 1 plays 1-2 combination with 3 players (short combination) switch positions.
Station 3: Player 1 dribbles, then passes to player 2. Player 2 passes into run of player 1 who is crossing over. Player 1 receives ball and dribbles again until player 2 overlaps. Taking short pass, player 2 dribbles

and passes into player 1's run. Player 2 makes run to finish final pass by player 1.

Station 4: 1 v 1 with neutral zone. Two players play 1 v 1. Player in possession of ball tries to beat defender and pass to teammate on other side of neutral zone.

PASSING

OBJECTIVE:	Improving passing and scoring
NUMBER OF PLAYERS:	20 (2 groups of 10)
AREA/FIELD:	Full field
TIME:	30 minutes
EQUIPMENT:	8 cones, 4 goals, supply of balls

ORGANIZATION:	• 2 players with ball next to goal. 4 players inside grid (15 yards x 25 yards) in between goals.
	• Players with ball play a long ball to players inside grid. They receive, dribble and shoot on goal.
INSTRUCTIONS:	Players switch position regularly.
COACHING POINTS:	• Player receiving ball must show for ball (movement).
	• Communicate and make eye contact.
	• Receive ball in direction of goal.
VARIATIONS:	Introduce defenders.

OBJECTIVE: Improving passing, 1-2 combination, dribbling and scoring

NUMBER OF PLAYERS: 4 per station

AREA/FIELD: Full field

TIME: 10 minutes per station

EQUIPMENT: 13 cones, 4 boards, goal, supply of balls

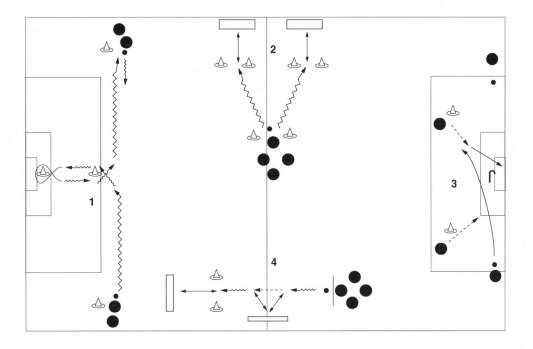

ORGANIZATION: Station 1: Player dribbles around cones and continues to other side. Player 2 takes over ball and repeats drill.
Station 2: Dribble and play 1-2 combination with board.
Station 3: Finish on goal from cross.
Station 4: Play 1-2 combination with board off the dribble.

Chapter 3

SHOOTING

SHOOTING 1

OBJECTIVE: Learning to shoot with instep

NUMBER OF PLAYERS: 6 - 12

AREA/FIELD: Third of field

TIME: 15 - 20 minutes

EQUIPMENT: Goal, supply of balls

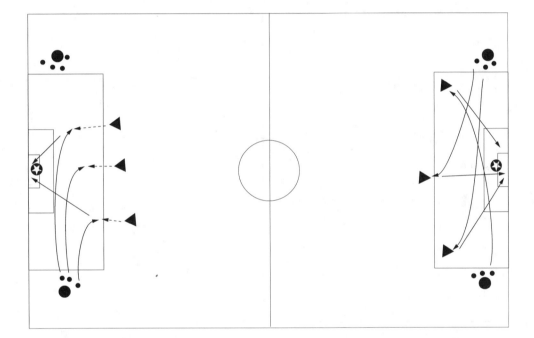

ORGANIZATION: Two feeders on outside of box. Cross balls to players on top of 18 yard box who shoot on goal.

INSTRUCTIONS:
• Put extra players behind goals to retrieve balls.
• Let players cross from left and right.

COACHING POINTS:
• Approach ball, don't wait for ball.
• Keep upper body over ball.
• Keep eyes on ball.
• Read flight of ball.

SHOOTING 2

OBJECTIVE:	Improving shooting at goal
NUMBER OF PLAYERS:	6 - 12
AREA/FIELD:	Half field
TIME:	30 minutes
EQUIPMENT:	3 cones, 3 goals, supply of balls

ORGANIZATION:	Start with shot on goal, move to cone and receive ball from goalkeeper. Dribble, shoot on goal, move around cone, receive ball from goalkeeper, dribble and shoot on goal.
INSTRUCTIONS:	Make sure goalkeeper has supply of balls for continuation of drill.
COACHING POINTS:	Look at goalkeeper's position before shooting.
VARIATIONS:	Go clockwise and counterclockwise.

SHOOTING 3

OBJECTIVE:	Improving shooting on the turn
NUMBER OF PLAYERS:	8 - 10
AREA/FIELD:	Half field
TIME:	15 minutes
EQUIPMENT:	4 cones, goal, supply of balls

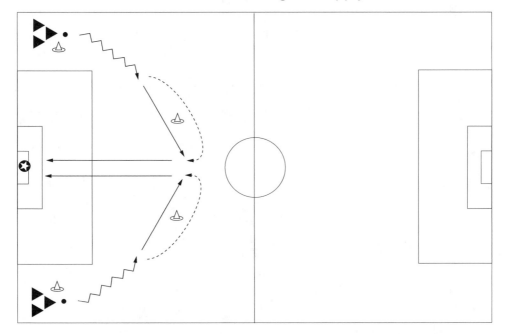

ORGANIZATION:	Players dribble from flank position toward cone. Approximately 5-6 yards before cone pass to inside of cone and make run around outside. Turn around cone and shoot at goal.
INSTRUCTIONS:	• Let players shoot from left and right. • Play the ball so it's ready to be shot on goal.
COACHING POINTS:	• Look at goalkeeper's position while turning. • Follow ball for rebounds.

SHOOTING 4

OBJECTIVE: Improving shooting after 1-2 combination

NUMBER OF PLAYERS: Groups of 3

AREA/FIELD: Half field

TIME: 10 - 15 minutes

EQUIPMENT: Supply of balls

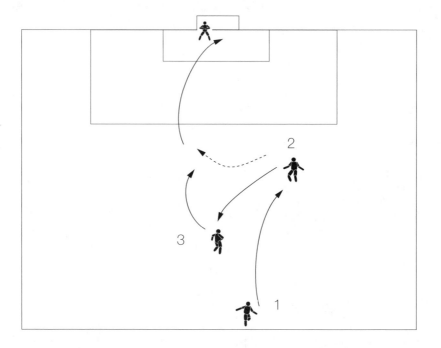

ORGANIZATION: Player 1 passes to player 2. Player 2 plays 1-2 combination with player 3. Player 2 turns to goal and finishes pass from player 3.

INSTRUCTIONS: Let players switch position after every shot (1 becomes 2, 2-3, 3-1).

COACHING POINTS:
- Play one touch.
- Turn quickly and finish.
- Shoot ball as played (don't take extra touches to settle ball).

SHOOTING 5

OBJECTIVE:	Improving shooting after long wallpass
NUMBER OF PLAYERS:	8 - 10 players
AREA/FIELD:	Half field
TIME:	15 - 20 minutes
EQUIPMENT:	Supply of balls

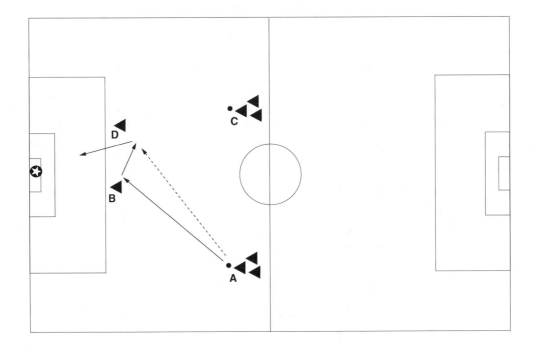

ORGANIZATION:	Player A plays long ball to player B. Follow pass and finish wallpass with shot on goal.
INSTRUCTIONS:	Player C passes to player D.
COACHING POINTS:	• Sprint/fast run to follow pass. • Strike ball at full speed.
VARIATIONS:	Let player B pass to player D who lays off ball to player A.

SHOOTING 6

OBJECTIVE:	Improving scoring
NUMBER OF PLAYERS:	10 - 12
AREA/FIELD:	Half field
TIME:	10 - 15 minutes
EQUIPMENT:	Supply of balls

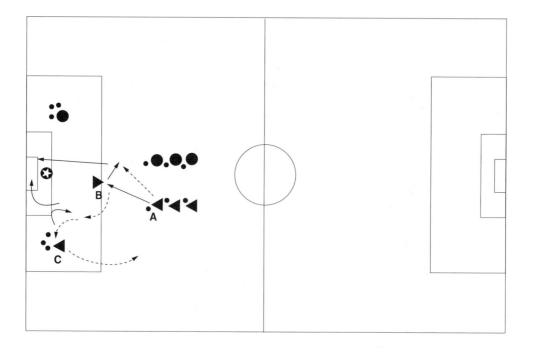

ORGANIZATION:	Players A and B play 1-2 combination. A shoots on goal. Player A then runs to six-yard box to head in cross from Player C.
INSTRUCTIONS:	Players switch position after every turn.
COACHING POINTS:	• Finish ball as quick as possible. • Head ball down.

SHOOTING 7

OBJECTIVE:	Learning to finish when fatigued.
NUMBER OF PLAYERS:	8 - 12
AREA/FIELD:	Full field
TIME:	15 - 20 minutes
EQUIPMENT:	6 cones, 3 hurdles (Dutch gates), 2 goals

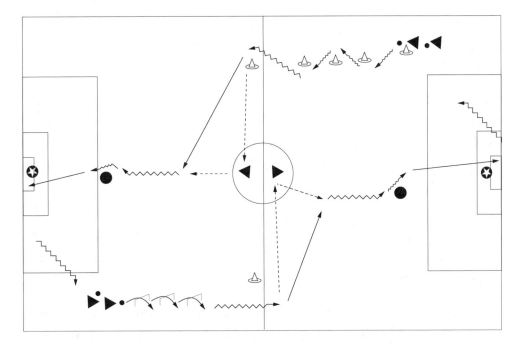

ORGANIZATION:	Players start dribble and hop over hurdles. At 1/2 field they play a wall pass with player in midfield. Players receive, dribble on, take on defenders and shoot.
INSTRUCTIONS:	• Let players start at same time. • If players don't score they become defenders.
COACHING POINTS:	• Make accurate pass into run. • Take on defenders with speed.

SHOOTING 8

OBJECTIVE: Learning to finish when fatigued

NUMBER OF PLAYERS: 8 - 12

AREA/FIELD: Full field

TIME: 10-15 minutes

EQUIPMENT: 4 cones, 2 goals, supply of balls

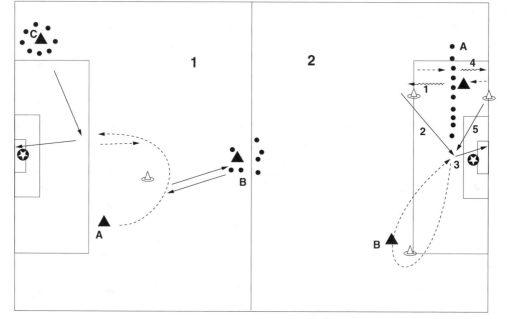

ORGANIZATION:
1. Player A runs to play a wallpass with player B. After wallpass run around cone and finish pass from player C.
2. Player A dribbles to end line, player B runs out, around cone and back to goal. Player A passes to player B. Player B shoots on goal.

COACHING POINTS:
- Look at goalkeeper's position before shooting. Don't slow down run to shoot.
- Read flight of ball and adjust position to score.

SHOOTING 9

OBJECTIVE: Improving scoring and sprinting

NUMBER OF PLAYERS: 4 - 8

AREA/FIELD: Half field

TIME: 10 - 15 minutes

EQUIPMENT: 2 cones, 1 goal, supply of balls

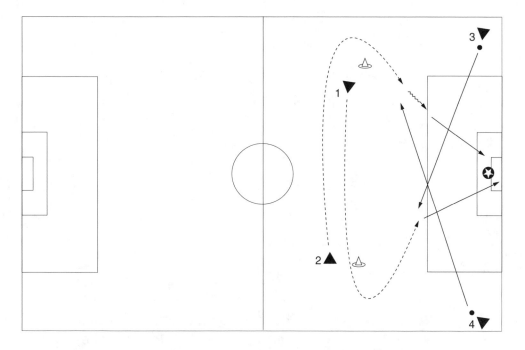

ORGANIZATION: Players 1 and 2 make run around cone and finish cross from players 3 and 4 respectively.

INSTRUCTIONS: Let player 2 start when player 1 has taken shot.

COACHING POINTS: • Read flight/path of the ball and adjust position to finish.
• Keep eye contact and communication between feeder and attacker.

SHOOTING

OBJECTIVE:	Improving finishing from cross
NUMBER OF PLAYERS:	8 - 10
AREA/FIELD:	Half field
TIME:	10 - 15 minutes
EQUIPMENT:	4 cones, goal, supply of balls

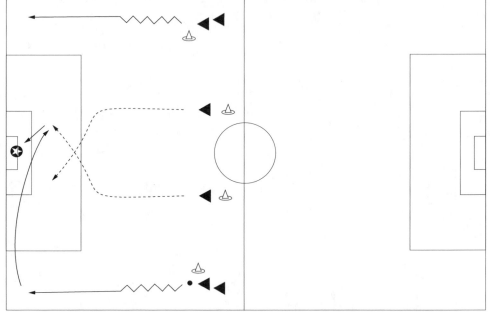

ORGANIZATION:	Player on flank makes run with ball and crosses ball to 2 attackers in front of goal.
INSTRUCTIONS:	Alternate left and right flank.
COACHING POINTS:	• Communication between flank players and attackers. • Cross over runs in front of goal (far player goes to near post, near player to far post).
VARIATIONS:	• Add defenders. • Add more attackers.

SHOOTING

11

OBJECTIVE: Learning to finish a cross

NUMBER OF PLAYERS: 6 - 10

AREA/FIELD: Half field

TIME: 15 - 20 minutes

EQUIPMENT: 4 cones, 2 goals, supply of balls

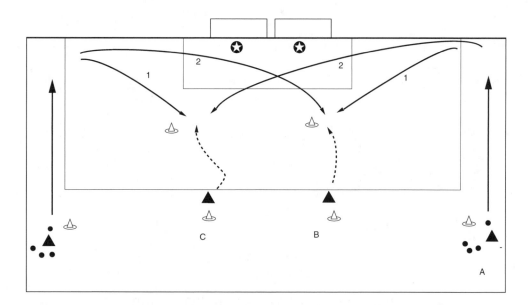

ORGANIZATION:
- Player A passes to self toward goalline.
- Player A crosses ball to 2 attackers in front of goal(low/high).

INSTRUCTIONS: Alternate cross from left and right.

COACHING POINTS:
- Pace ball correctly so player can cross the ball without stopping or touching the ball.
- Low cross; hard and accurate.
- Time the runs to finish on goal.

SHOOTING

OBJECTIVE:	Learning to finish after 1 v 1
NUMBER OF PLAYERS:	8 - 12
AREA/FIELD:	Full field
TIME:	10 - 15 minutes
EQUIPMENT:	8 cones, 2 goals, supply of balls

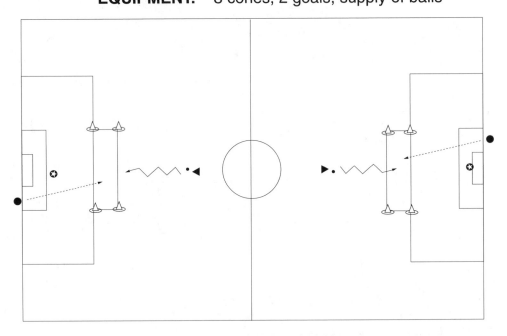

ORGANIZATION:	Player A dribbles towards zone. Player B (defender) runs toward zone to defend player A. Player A attempts to beat defender and score.
INSTRUCTIONS:	Let attacker and defender switch position if defender wins ball. Shot cannot be taken until player A reaches the zone.
COACHING POINTS:	Dribble toward zone with speed. If defender is late, shoot early.

SHOOTING   13

OBJECTIVE:	Learning to score under pressure
NUMBER OF PLAYERS:	8 - 12
AREA/FIELD:	Full field
TIME:	15 - 20 minutes
EQUIPMENT:	6 cones, 2 goals, supply of balls

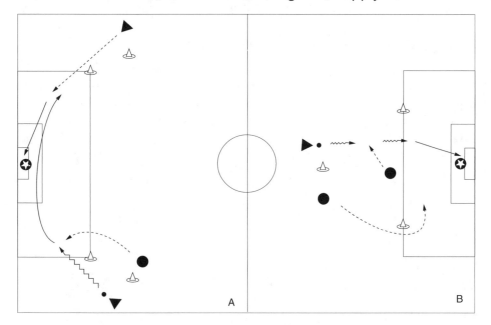

ORGANIZATION: A: Flank player, under pressure of defender, tries to cross ball to incoming forward under pressure of defender.

B: Attacker takes on defender and tries to score. Second defender puts pressure on from side.

COACHING POINTS: A: Flank player doesn't need to beat defender. Cross as soon as possible. Maintain eye contact and communication.

B: Finish as quickly as possible. Don't let defenders get organized.

SHOOTING 14

OBJECTIVE:	Learning to finish a cross
NUMBER OF PLAYERS:	10 - 12
AREA/FIELD:	Full field
TIME:	15 - 20 minutes
EQUIPMENT:	16 cones, 2 goals, supply of balls

ORGANIZATION: Player A takes on player B. After beating B, crosses ball to attackers in front of goal.

COACHING POINTS:
- Cross ball as quickly as possible.
- Forward needs to be in motion, drawing defender out of position.
- Move to position where you can run onto cross.

VARIATIONS: Instead of 1 v 1, play 2 v 2 on flank and in front of goal.

SHOOTING 15

OBJECTIVE:	Learning to cross or finish after 1 v 1
NUMBER OF PLAYERS:	10 -14
AREA/FIELD:	Full field
TIME:	15 - 20 minutes
EQUIPMENT:	10 cones, 2 goals , supply of balls

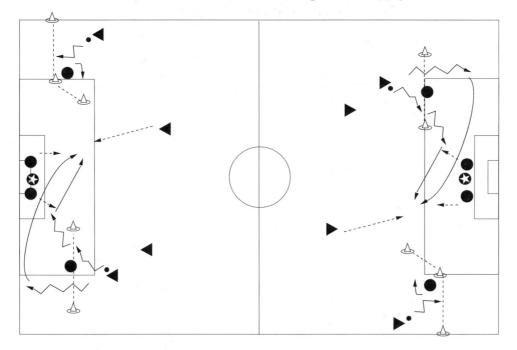

ORGANIZATION:	Attacker takes on defender and crosses ball to teammate or shoots at goal. After defender has been beaten 2 defenders defend inside box.
COACHING POINTS:	• If attacker beats defender to outside, cross.
	• If attacker beats defender to inside, shoot or pass to teammate.

SHOOTING   16

OBJECTIVE: Learning to cross and finish under pressure

NUMBER OF PLAYERS: 12 - 16

AREA/FIELD: Full field

TIME: 15 - 20 minutes

EQUIPMENT: 6 cones, 2 goals, supply of balls

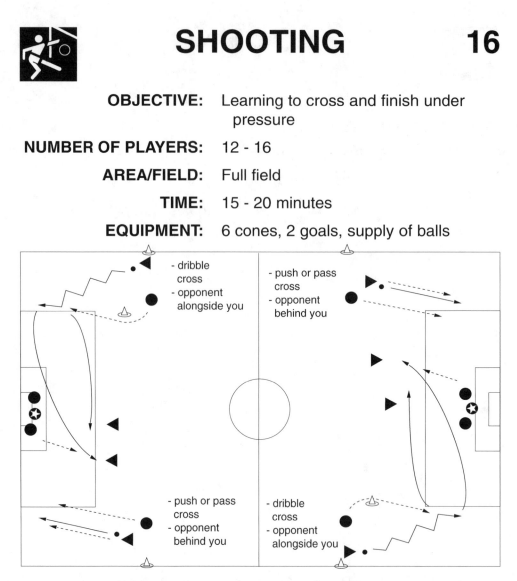

- dribble cross
- opponent alongside you

- push or pass cross
- opponent behind you

- push or pass cross
- opponent behind you

- dribble cross
- opponent alongside you

ORGANIZATION: Attacker and defender play 1 v 1 on flank. After beating defender cross to 2 attackers defended by 2 defenders (coming from inside 6 yard box).

INSTRUCTIONS: Let defenders and attackers switch positions frequently.

COACHING POINTS:
- Cross as quickly as possible.
- Two attackers cross over (near and far post).
- Keep attackers in motion.

SHOOTING 17

OBJECTIVE: Learning to finish a cross and shooting from 18 yards

NUMBER OF PLAYERS: 6 - 12

AREA/FIELD: Half field

TIME: 10 - 15 minutes

EQUIPMENT: 4 cones, goal, supply of balls

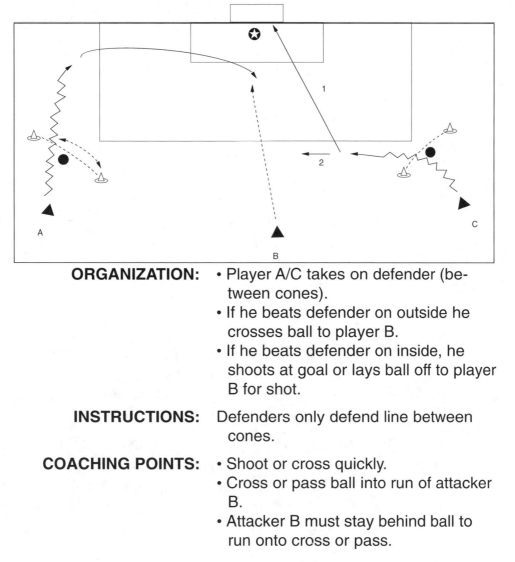

ORGANIZATION:
- Player A/C takes on defender (between cones).
- If he beats defender on outside he crosses ball to player B.
- If he beats defender on inside, he shoots at goal or lays ball off to player B for shot.

INSTRUCTIONS: Defenders only defend line between cones.

COACHING POINTS:
- Shoot or cross quickly.
- Cross or pass ball into run of attacker B.
- Attacker B must stay behind ball to run onto cross or pass.

SHOOTING 18

OBJECTIVE:	Learning to finish from cross
NUMBER OF PLAYERS:	6 - 12
AREA/FIELD:	Third of field
TIME:	15 - 20 minutes
EQUIPMENT:	12 cones, 2 goals, supply of balls

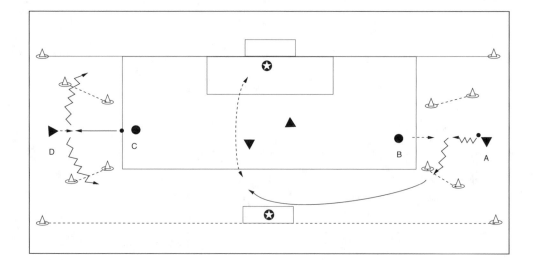

ORGANIZATION:	• Players A and D take on defenders B and C to left or right. • After crossing line between cones, cross to attackers in front of goal.
INSTRUCTIONS:	Players A and D alternate crosses.
COACHING POINTS:	• Use left and right side to take on defender/fake out defender. • Attacker in front of goal must stay behind ball.

SHOOTING 19

OBJECTIVE: Improving passing and shooting from dribble

NUMBER OF PLAYERS: 8 - 12

AREA/FIELD: Full field

TIME: 15 - 20 minutes

EQUIPMENT: 2 goals, supply of balls

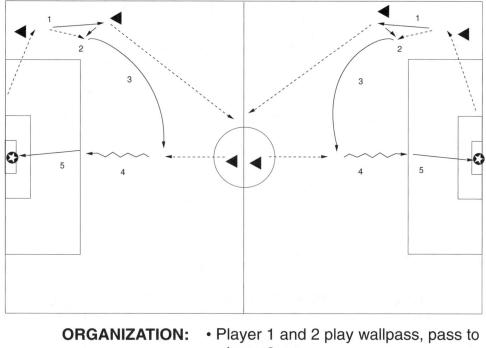

ORGANIZATION:
- Player 1 and 2 play wallpass, pass to player 3.
- Player 3 dribbles to 18 yard line and takes shot on goal.

INSTRUCTIONS: Let players switch position

COACHING POINTS:
- Pass into player C run/path.
- Dribble with speed.
- Shoot from dribble.

VARIATIONS: Introduce defenders.

SHOOTING 20

OBJECTIVE:	Improving scoring from cross and runs to near and far post
NUMBER OF PLAYERS:	12 - 14
AREA/FIELD:	Full field
TIME:	15 - 20 minutes
EQUIPMENT:	Supply of balls, 2 goals

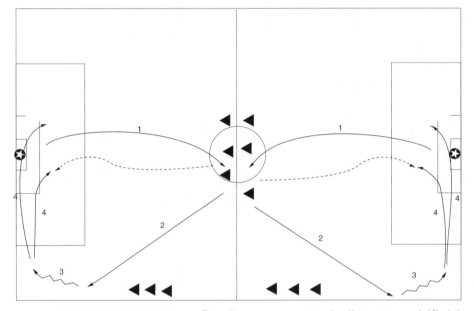

ORGANIZATION:	Goalkeeper punts ball out to midfield. Player 1 receives ball and passes to flank player 2. Player 2 dribbles to endline and crosses ball to player 1.
INSTRUCTIONS:	Crosses from right and left flank.
COACHING POINTS:	• Player 1 needs to stay behind the ball. • Player 1 has the option to make far and near post run. • Make eye contact and communication.
VARIATIONS:	Introduce defenders.

SHOOTING 21

OBJECTIVE: Improving scoring from cross

NUMBER OF PLAYERS: 10 - 12

AREA/FIELD: Half field

TIME: 15 - 20 minutes

EQUIPMENT: 1 goal, supply of balls

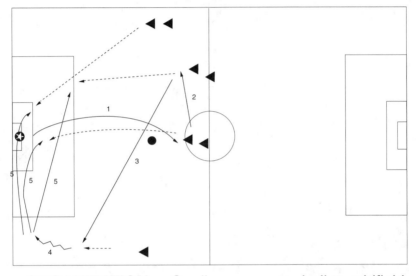

ORGANIZATION: Goalkeeper punts ball to midfield. Player 1 receives ball and passes short to player 2. Player 2 gives a crosspass to player 3. Player 3 dribbles to endline and has 3 options; Cross to near or far post or pass to top of 18 yard box.

INSTRUCTIONS: Let players switch frequently.

COACHING POINTS: • Make passes and crosses into runs of players.
• Attackers make cross over runs to cover near and far post.
• Player 2 covers position on top of 18 yard line to shoot at goal.

SHOOTING

OBJECTIVE: Learning to score after 1 v 1

NUMBER OF PLAYERS: 14 - 16

AREA/FIELD: Full field

TIME: 20 - 25 minutes

EQUIPMENT: Supply of balls, 2 goals

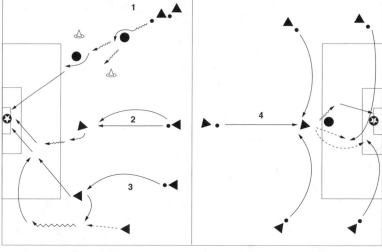

ORGANIZATION:

1: Attacker takes on 2 defenders and shoots on goal.

2: Attacker receives high or low pass, turn with ball and shoot.

3: Attacker receives pass, and wallpass to flank and finish cross or turns with ball and shoots at goal.

4: Shooting a series of 5 balls under pressure of defender 4 crosses plus 1 pass from midfield.

INSTRUCTIONS:

Let all players play all positions (offense and defense).

COACHING POINTS:

• Make accurate passes and crosses.
• Everyone communicates.
• Finish with determination.

94

SHOOTING 23

OBJECTIVE: Learning to finish of the dribble on the counter attack

NUMBER OF PLAYERS: 10 - 12

AREA/FIELD: Full field

TIME: 15 - 20 minutes

EQUIPMENT: Supply of balls, 2 goals

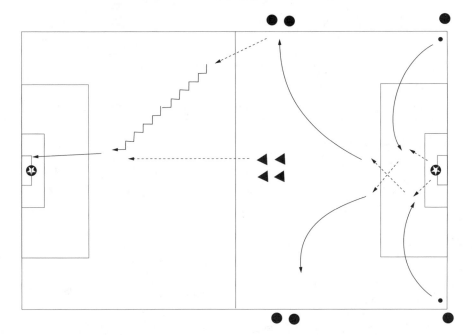

ORGANIZATION:
- Two players take corners. Goalkeeper intercepts ball and throws out ball quickly to player on flank.
- Flank player receives ball and dribbles quickly under pressure of defender to score in opposite goal.

INSTRUCTIONS:
- Give inswinging and outswinging corners.
- Start drill from both sides of field (both goals).

SHOOTING

COACHING POINTS:
- Start run as soon as goalkeeper catches ball.
- Receive ball in direction of goal (opposition's goal).
- Execute counter at speed.
- Cut off defenders' angle of retreat.

Chapter 4

HEADING

HEADING 1

OBJECTIVE:	Improving heading skills
NUMBER OF PLAYERS:	Groups of 4
TIME:	5 - 10 minutes
EQUIPMENT:	Supply of balls

1

groups of 4

2

4 times left
4 times right

3

4 times left
4 times right

ORGANIZATION: 1: Attacker heads ball back to 2 feeders under pressure of defender.

2: Attacker makes run and checks back under pressure of defender. Player 1 throws ball to attacker who heads ball to player 2.

3: Player 1 throws ball to attacker over defender or in front of defender, so attacker needs to come around defender.

COACHING POINTS: • Head ball down to teammates' feet.
• Keep communication and eye contact between feeder and header.

HEADING 2

OBJECTIVE:	Improving heading technique
NUMBER OF PLAYERS:	Groups of 3
TIME:	5 - 10 minutes
EQUIPMENT:	2 cones, 2 balls

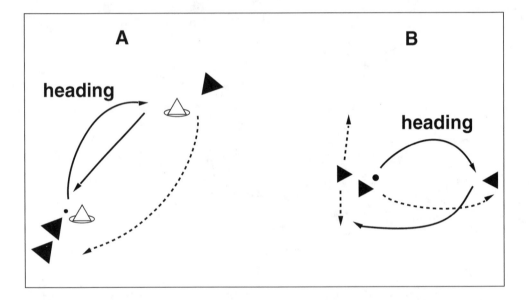

ORGANIZATION: A: Player 1 throws ball to player 2. Player 2 heads ball to ground and follows ball with run.

B: Player 1 throws ball to player 2. Player 2 heads ball to player 3 who makes run.

COACHING POINTS:
- Start run immediately after landing on both feet.
- Head down to feet.
- Use "throw in" throw.

HEADING   3

OBJECTIVE:	Improving heading skills
NUMBER OF PLAYERS:	Groups of 3
TIME:	5 - 10 minutes
EQUIPMENT:	3 balls

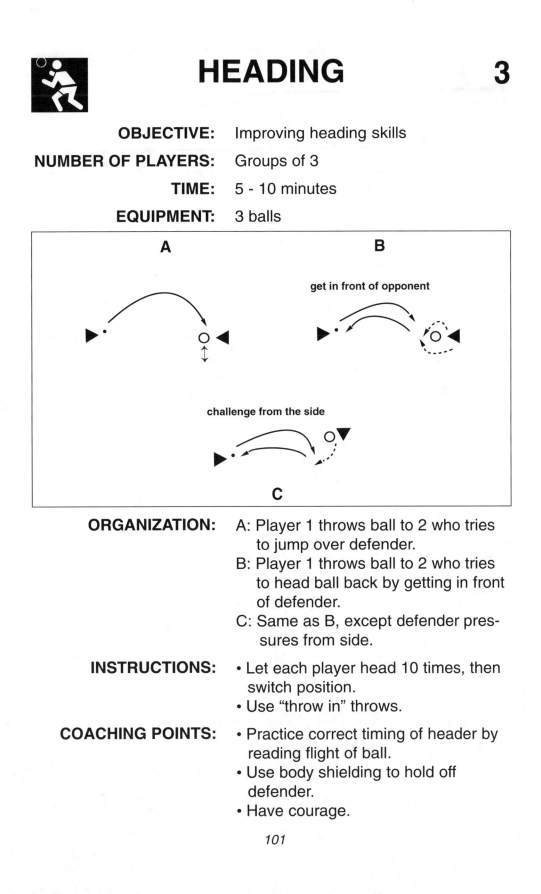

ORGANIZATION:
A: Player 1 throws ball to 2 who tries to jump over defender.
B: Player 1 throws ball to 2 who tries to head ball back by getting in front of defender.
C: Same as B, except defender pressures from side.

INSTRUCTIONS:
• Let each player head 10 times, then switch position.
• Use "throw in" throws.

COACHING POINTS:
• Practice correct timing of header by reading flight of ball.
• Use body shielding to hold off defender.
• Have courage.

HEADING

3

VARIATIONS: Competitive game between defender and attacker; who wins the most head balls.

HEADING 4

OBJECTIVE: Improving heading to teammate and scoring

NUMBER OF PLAYERS: Groups of 3 or more

TIME: 5 - 10 min.

EQUIPMENT: 2 goals, supply of balls

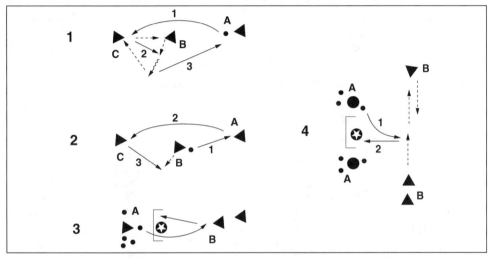

ORGANIZATION:
1. Player A feeds ball to player C who heads ball into player B's run.
2. Player B feeds ball to player A. Player A heads ball to player C who heads ball into run of player B.
3. Player A feeds ball to player B who heads ball at goal to score (player A behind goal).
4. Player A feeds ball from side of goal to incoming player B.

COACHING POINTS:
• Get over ball to hit top half of ball(heading down).
• Position body behind ball.

VARIATIONS: Introduce defenders.

HEADING 5

OBJECTIVE: Improving heading on goal

NUMBER OF PLAYERS: 10 - 12

AREA/FIELD: 50 yards x 60 yards

TIME: 10 - 15 minutes

EQUIPMENT: 2 goals, supply of balls

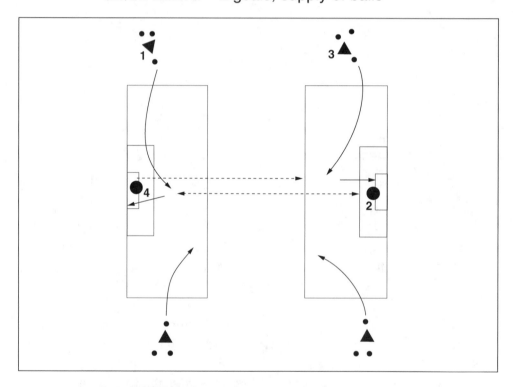

ORGANIZATION: Player 1 crosses ball to incoming player 2. Player 2 heads ball on goal. Repeat with players 3 and 4.

INSTRUCTIONS:
- Crosses from left and right.
- Inswinging and outswinging crosses.
- High and low crosses.

COACHING POINTS:
- Read flight of ball and time runs.
- Head ball down to corners of goal.

HEADING 6

OBJECTIVE:	Improving heading on goal from cross(under pressure of defender)
NUMBER OF PLAYERS:	12 - 16
AREA/FIELD:	Half field
TIME:	10 - 15 minutes
EQUIPMENT:	2 cones, goal, supply of balls

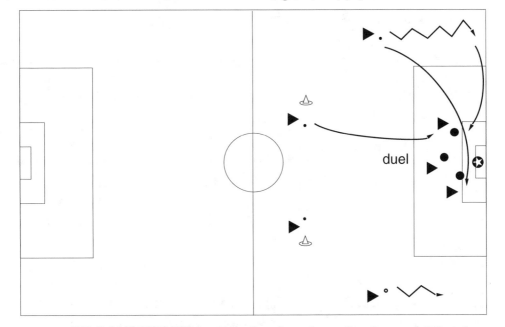

ORGANIZATION:	Two feeders from flanks and 2 feeders from midfield serve crosses into 18 yard box where 3 attackers and 3 defenders are positioned. Attackers attempt to score on goal.
COACHING POINTS:	• Don't get too close to goal. • Keep all attackers moving. • Near and far post run.
VARIATIONS:	Use corner kicks and free .kicks to cross balls.

HEADING

OBJECTIVE: Improving heading skills in 3 v 3 game.

NUMBER OF PLAYERS: 9 plus goalkeeper

AREA/FIELD: Half field

TIME: 10 - 15 minutes

EQUIPMENT: 6 flags, 1 goal, supply of balls

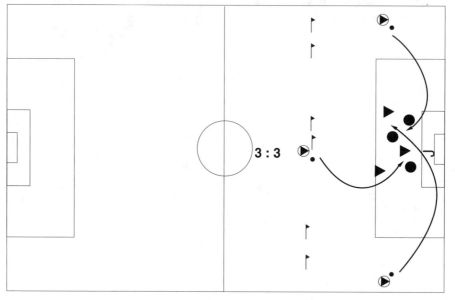

ORGANIZATION:
- Three attackers and 3 defenders play 3 v 3 inside box.
- Three feeders serve crosses. Defenders can score by heading on 3 small goals on 30 yard line. Attackers can score by heading on goal.

INSTRUCTIONS: Switch attackers, defenders and feeders after 10-15 crosses.

COACHING POINTS:
- Stress movement/runs by attackers.
- Defenders direct their defensive headers towards 3 small goals.

VARIATIONS: Use 2 goals plus 2 goalkeepers.

HEADING 8

OBJECTIVE:	Improving heading skills in small sided game
NUMBER OF PLAYERS:	Teams of 3
AREA/FIELD:	20 yards x 10 yards
TIME:	5 - 10 minutes
EQUIPMENT:	4 cones, supply of balls

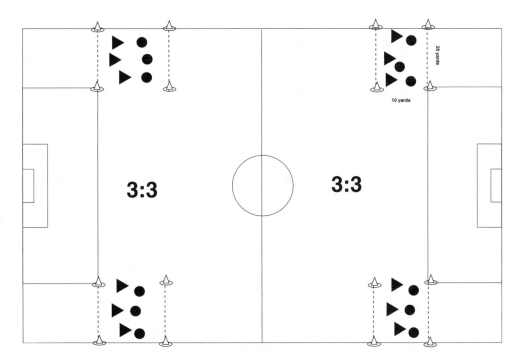

ORGANIZATION:	• Two teams of 3 play a heading game. • A team can score by passing the ball with their heads into teammates' hands behind line.
INSTRUCTIONS:	• Only use hands to catch at waist height or throw up the ball to head pass it. • Players can't run with ball.

HEADING 8

COACHING POINTS: • Communicate.
• Stress movement of the ball.
• Keep eyes open.
• Use forehead to head ball.

VARIATIONS: • Use more players.
• Adjust size of field.

HEADING

OBJECTIVE: Improving heading on goal from crosses

NUMBER OF PLAYERS: 10

AREA/FIELD: Half field

TIME: 15 - 20 minutes

EQUIPMENT: 2 goals, supply of balls

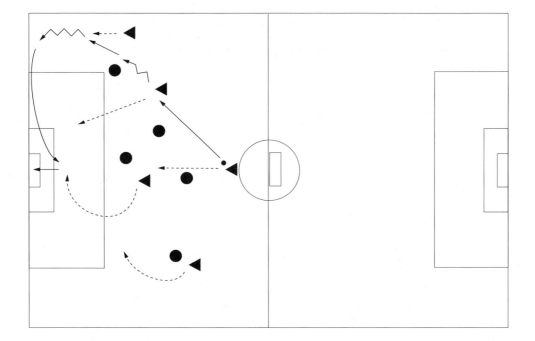

ORGANIZATION: Two teams of 5 players play on 1/2 field with 2 goals (NO goalkeepers). Players can score only by heading.

INSTRUCTIONS: Start game off with low pressure from defenders.

COACHING POINTS: • Build up over flanks.
• Make runs to near and far post.

VARIATIONS: Introduce goalkeeper.

Chapter 5

RESTART PLAYS

RESTART PLAYS 1

OBJECTIVE:	Scoring from freekick
NUMBER OF PLAYERS:	22
AREA/FIELD:	Full Field
EQUIPMENT:	Supply of balls

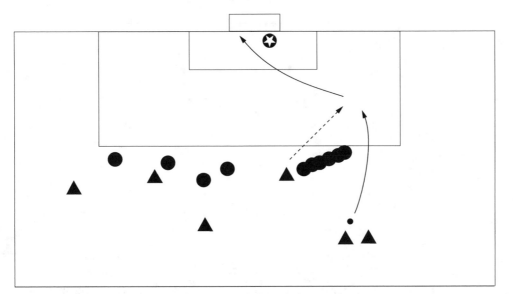

ORGANIZATION:	• Two attackers with ball, 1 attacker on side of wall.
	• Ball is played to outside of wall. Attacker on inside of wall makes a run behind wall into path of ball.
	• Player turns and shoots at goal out of turn.
INSTRUCTIONS:	• Let all players (offense and defense) play game-like.
	• Cover ALL positions.
COACHING POINTS:	• If freekick is from right side of goal, let a left-footed player fake the kick as distraction.
	• Right-footed player makes pass.

OBJECTIVE: Scoring from cornerkick

NUMBER OF PLAYERS: 22

AREA/FIELD: Full field

EQUIPMENT: Supply of balls

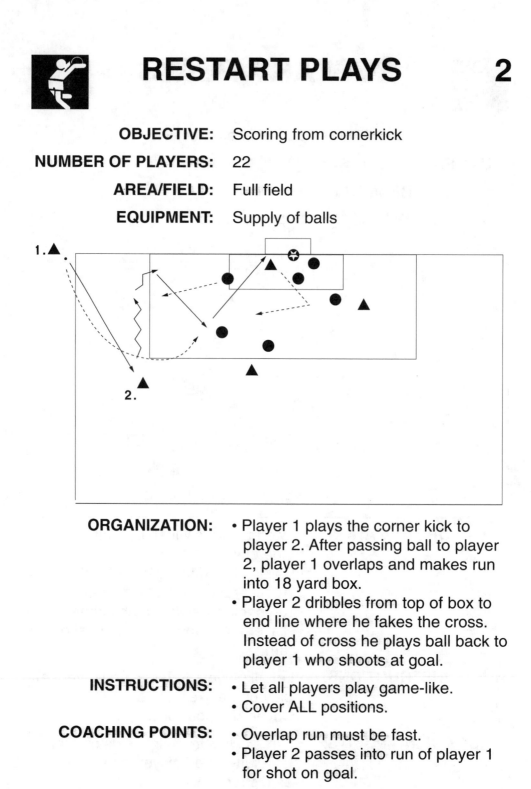

ORGANIZATION:
- Player 1 plays the corner kick to player 2. After passing ball to player 2, player 1 overlaps and makes run into 18 yard box.
- Player 2 dribbles from top of box to end line where he fakes the cross. Instead of cross he plays ball back to player 1 who shoots at goal.

INSTRUCTIONS:
- Let all players play game-like.
- Cover ALL positions.

COACHING POINTS:
- Overlap run must be fast.
- Player 2 passes into run of player 1 for shot on goal.

VARIATIONS: Play "live" game after cornerkick.

RESTART PLAYS

OBJECTIVE: Scoring from corner

NUMBER OF PLAYERS: 22

AREA/FIELD: Full field

EQUIPMENT: Supply of balls

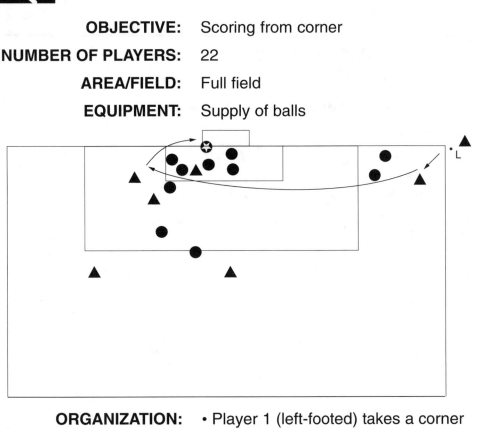

ORGANIZATION:
- Player 1 (left-footed) takes a corner from right. He passes ball short to player 2 who stops ball.
- Player 1 runs onto ball and crosses ball from wider angle to teammate at far corner who heads on goal.

INSTRUCTIONS: Right-footed player from left.

COACHING POINTS:
- Draw defenders out of box to create space in front of goal.
- Watch off-side.
- Make blind-side runs.
- Near and far post runs.
- Cross out of reach of goalkeeper.

VARIATIONS: Play live game after corner.

RESTART PLAYS   4

OBJECTIVE:	Scoring from corner
NUMBER OF PLAYERS:	22
AREA/FIELD:	Full field
EQUIPMENT:	Supply of balls

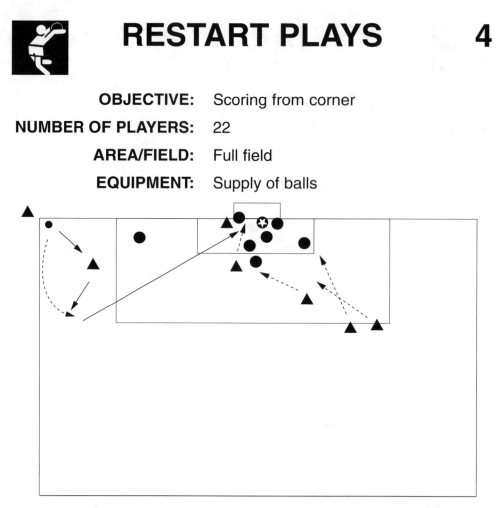

ORGANIZATION: Players 1 and 2 play short corner. Player 1 ends up with ball at top of 18 yard box. He takes a shot at waist height to near post.

INSTRUCTIONS:
• Let all players play game-like.
• Cover all positions.

COACHING POINTS:
• Passes to be accurate and with pace.
• Other attackers start movement runs before shot has been taken.
• Attackers collapse inside box.
• Distract goalkeeper.
• Watch off-side trap.

RESTART PLAYS 5

OBJECTIVE:	Scoring from corner
NUMBER OF PLAYERS:	22
AREA/FIELD:	Full field
EQUIPMENT:	Supply of balls

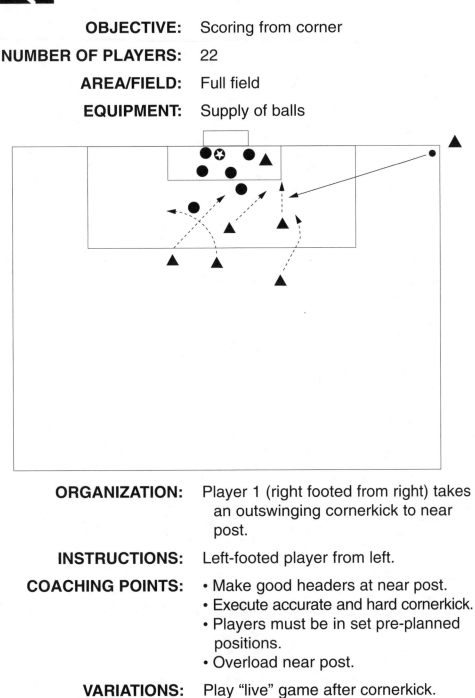

ORGANIZATION:	Player 1 (right footed from right) takes an outswinging cornerkick to near post.
INSTRUCTIONS:	Left-footed player from left.
COACHING POINTS:	• Make good headers at near post. • Execute accurate and hard cornerkick. • Players must be in set pre-planned positions. • Overload near post.
VARIATIONS:	Play "live" game after cornerkick.

Chapter 6

GOALKEEPING

GOALKEEPING

OBJECTIVE:	Goalkeeper squash
NUMBER OF PLAYERS:	2
AREA/FIELD:	10 yards x 10 yards
TIME:	10 - 15 minutes
EQUIPMENT:	6 cones, 1 kick-back rebounder, 1 ball

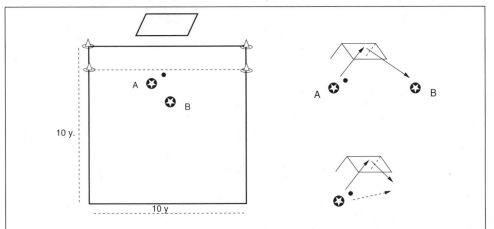

Goalkeeper squash

ORGANIZATION:	Two goalkeepers are positioned inside a 10 x 10 grid. They attempt to score by throwing ball into kick-back rebounder to bounce back out of reach of other goalkeeper inside grid.
INSTRUCTIONS:	If goalkeeper catches ball before it hits ground, he throws it back from that spot.
COACHING POINTS:	• Stay on toes at all times, ready to move and adjust. • Concentrate!
VARIATIONS:	• Four players (2 v 2). • Catch ball with 1 hand. • Throw only with weaker arm.

GOALKEEPING 2

OBJECTIVE:	Improving throwing and catching
NUMBER OF PLAYERS:	4 - 8
AREA/FIELD:	15 yards x 25 yards
TIME:	10 - 15 minutes
EQUIPMENT:	Two kick-back rebounders, 6 cones, 1 ball

"Kick back" 1

center line

25 y

"Kick back" 2

15 y

"Kick back" game

ORGANIZATION: Team in possession passes the ball around (using hands) and attempts to cross center line. After crossing center field they attempt to throw ball into kick-back to score.

INSTRUCTIONS:
- Teammate has to catch ball after it comes back from kick-back and before it touches the ground.
- If other team intercepts ball, it has to go back over center field before they can score.
- Players can't run with ball.

GOALKEEPING 3

OBJECTIVE:	Learning to punch ball
NUMBER OF PLAYERS:	10 - 12
AREA/FIELD:	40 yards x 20 yards
TIME:	15 - 20 minutes
EQUIPMENT:	4 cones, 2 goals, supply of balls

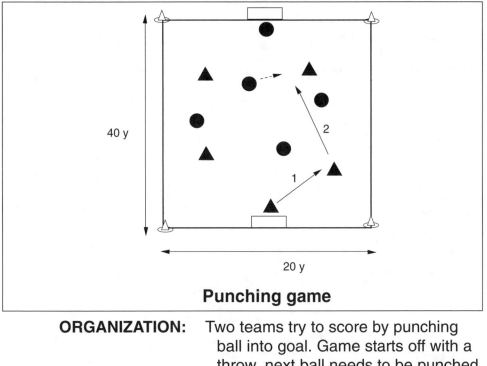

Punching game

ORGANIZATION:	Two teams try to score by punching ball into goal. Game starts off with a throw, next ball needs to be punched. Third can be caught again. Players can move around freely.
INSTRUCTIONS:	• If ball touches ground, ball turns over to other team.
	• All players (goalkeepers's) must shout for ball ("keepers ball"), otherwise ball turns over.
	• Keeper in goal is allowed to catch ball.

GOALKEEPING 3

COACHING POINTS: • Punch ball at highest points.
  • Direct punch to keep possession.

GOALKEEPING 4

OBJECTIVE: Improving catching and throwing with keeper volleyball

NUMBER OF PLAYERS: 8 - 10

AREA/FIELD: 20 yards x 15 yards

TIME: 15 - 20 minutes

EQUIPMENT: 4 cones, volleyball net, 1 ball

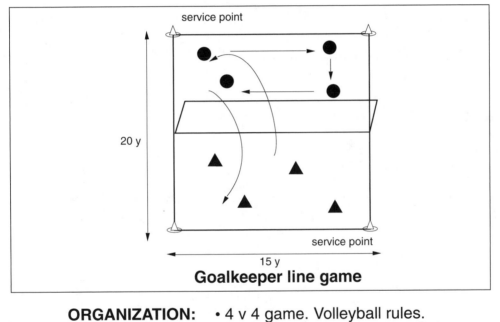

Goalkeeper line game

ORGANIZATION:
- 4 v 4 game. Volleyball rules.
- Game starts with throw as service. First ball may be caught. Other passes must be punched.

INSTRUCTIONS:
- Points are scored when ball bounces on ground.
- Ball must be played 3 times before going over net.

COACHING POINTS:
- Use 1 or 2 hands for punches.
- Time your jump and punch.
- Communicate.

GOALKEEPING 5

OBJECTIVE: Improving catching and throwing
Goalie War

NUMBER OF PLAYERS: 2

AREA/FIELD: 12 yards x 20 yards

TIME: 10 - 15 minutes

EQUIPMENT: 6 cones, 2 goals, 1 ball

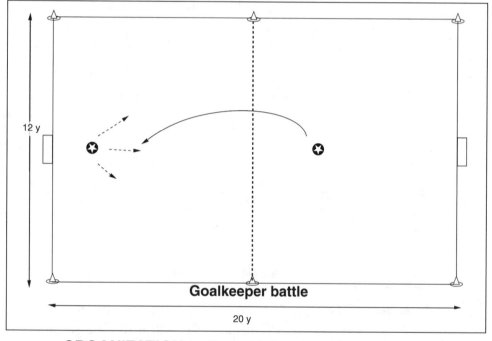

Goalkeeper battle

12 y

20 y

ORGANIZATION: Two goalkeepers both defend a half field and a goal. Goalkeepers try to score by throwing ball into opponent's goal from own half of field.

INSTRUCTIONS:
- Goalkeeper may throw ball from spot where he catches it.
- Game starts from goalline.
- When ball is out-of-bounds, start from goalline.

GOALKEEPING 5

COACHING POINTS:
- Be ready to adjust and change position quickly.
- Throw accurately.

VARIATIONS:
- Score by volley, drop-kick or shot.
- Throw with weaker arm.
- Use 4 goals/extra goalkeepers.

GOALKEEPING 6

OBJECTIVE: Improving catching and throwing

NUMBER OF PLAYERS: 8 - 12

AREA/FIELD: 40 yards x 20 yards

TIME: 15 - 20 minutes

EQUIPMENT: 8 cones, 1 ball

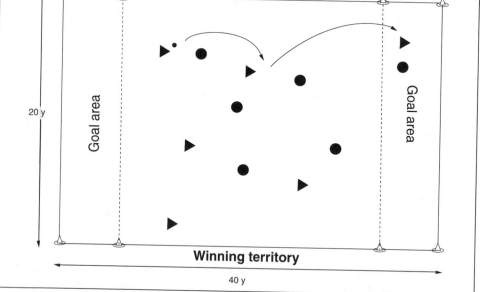

ORGANIZATION: Two teams try to score by throwing ball to teammate inside marked-off goal area.

INSTRUCTIONS:
- Pass by throwing ball.
- Ball can't touch ground.
- Players can't run with ball.
- Players can't be in goal area unless ball is played to them.

COACHING POINTS:
- Make quick and accurate passes.
- Communicate and keep eye contact.

VARIATIONS: Use volleys instead of throws.

GOALKEEPING 7

OBJECTIVE:	Improving catching and punting
NUMBER OF PLAYERS:	2
AREA/FIELD:	Grids 12 yards x 12 yards, distance between grids is 40 yards
TIME:	10 minutes
EQUIPMENT:	8 cones, 1 ball

---

40 yards

Goalkeeper game

ORGANIZATION:	Players A and B each defend a grid. They try to score by punting the ball into the opponent's grid. If ball bounces inside grid, player scores points. Other player can prevent bounce by catching ball.
INSTRUCTIONS:	• Score from volley: 1 point. • Score from drop-kick: 2 points. • Ball outside grid: 1 point opponent.
COACHING POINTS:	• Punt accurately: concentrate. • Put good pace and direction on ball. • Use instep/laces.
VARIATIONS:	Vary distance and size of grids.

GOALKEEPING 8

OBJECTIVE:	Improving goalkeeping skills in open field
NUMBER OF PLAYERS:	8 - 12
AREA/FIELD:	20 yards x 50 yards
TIME:	10 - 15 minutes
EQUIPMENT:	6 cones, 2 goals, supply of balls

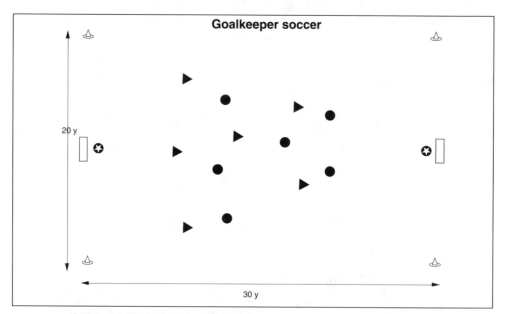

Goalkeeper soccer

ORGANIZATION:	• Two teams try to score on goals. • Team in possession plays "regular" soccer. • Defending team uses "Goalkeeper skills" (e.g diving, catching, etc.) to win ball back.
INSTRUCTIONS:	Both teams have permanent goalkeeper in goal.
COACHING POINTS:	• Practice quick transitions. • Utilize quick hands and feet. • Don't go to ground too quickly.

GOALKEEPING 9

OBJECTIVE:	Improving pick-up and distribution
NUMBER OF PLAYERS:	6
AREA/FIELD:	Half field
TIME:	10 minutes
EQUIPMENT:	6 cones, supply of balls

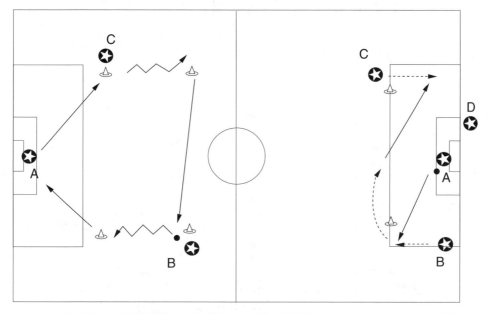

ORGANIZATION:	Player B dribbles and passes ball back to goalkeeper. Goalkeeper quickly picks up ball and rolls or throws ball to moving player C.
INSTRUCTIONS:	Pass and roll (distribution) to both sides.
COACHING POINTS:	• Stay behind ball when picking up. • Distribute into players' run. • Keep ball close to ground. • Bend knees when rolling/distributing ball.
VARIATIONS:	Throws or punts to players.

GOALKEEPING   10

OBJECTIVE:	Improving quick transition by goal-keeping
NUMBER OF PLAYERS:	8 - 10
AREA/FIELD:	Full field
TIME:	15 - 20 minutes
EQUIPMENT:	Supply of balls

ORGANIZATION:	Player crosses ball inside 18 yard box. Goalkeeper intercepts (catches) ball and starts attack quickly by punting ball upfield to 2 attackers. Attackers play 2 v 2 against 2 defenders and try to score on opposite goal.
INSTRUCTIONS:	Start game on other side after attack.
COACHING POINTS:	• Look up quickly after catching ball; Vision. • Pass/punt into space or run of attacker. • Concentrate on accurate pass.
VARIATIONS:	Play 3 v 3, 4 v 4.

GOALKEEPING 11

OBJECTIVE:	Improving collection of crosses and accuracy of distribution
NUMBER OF PLAYERS:	1 - 4
AREA/FIELD:	Half field
TIME:	15 minutes
EQUIPMENT:	4 goals, supply of balls

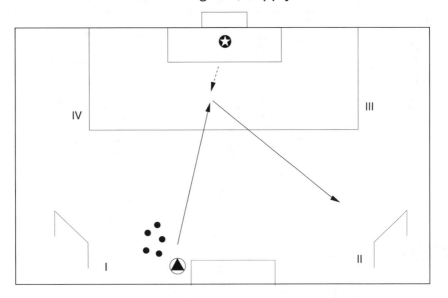

ORGANIZATION:	Coach sends in crosses to goalkeeper from various positions (I, II, III, IV). Goalkeeper intercepts crosses and starts attack quickly by throwing or punting ball in 1 of 3 goals.
INSTRUCTIONS:	Vary crosses; in/out swinging, hard, low.
COACHING POINTS:	Decide quickly where to throw or punt ball.
VARIATIONS:	Read flight/trajectory of ball. Put goalkeepers in all 4 goals.

OBJECTIVE: Improving communication and teamwork between goalkeeper and defender

NUMBER OF PLAYERS: 3 - 8

AREA/FIELD: Half field

TIME: 20 - 25 minutes

EQUIPMENT: 4 goals, 2 cones, supply of balls

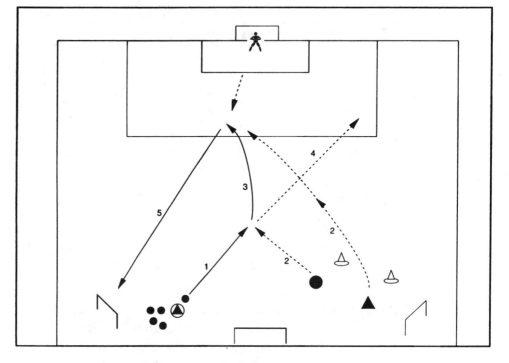

ORGANIZATION: Coach plays ball into space between goalkeeper and defender (pressured by an attacker). Defender and goalkeeper try to clear ball or try to keep possession by working together. They can score in 1 of 3 goals at half field.

INSTRUCTIONS: If attacker wins ball, he can shoot on goal.

GOALKEEPING 12

COACHING POINTS:
- Quick and decisive coaching between goalkeeper and defender.
- Accurate passing to keep possesion or try to score.
- Read path of ball.

GOALKEEPING 13

OBJECTIVE: Improving judgement, communication, positioning and responsibilities

NUMBER OF PLAYERS: 4 - 8

AREA/FIELD: Half field

TIME: 15 - 20 minutes

EQUIPMENT: 3 cones, 4 goals, supply of balls

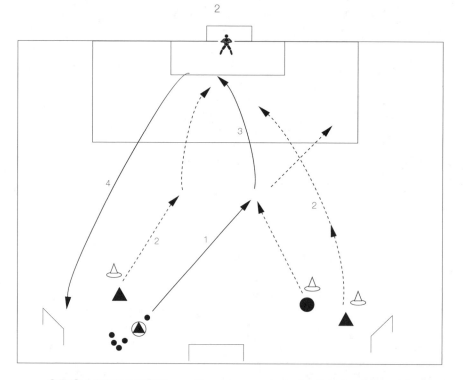

ORGANIZATION: Coach passes ball into space between defender and goalkeeper. Two attackers on either side try to win ball and score. Goalkeeper and defender try to gain possession of ball and score in 1 of 3 goals.

INSTRUCTIONS: Vary pass; pace, direction and height.

GOALKEEPING 13

COACHING POINTS:
- Communication between goalkeeper and defender.
- Make quick transition when winning possession.
- Goalkeeper comes off line and finds position quickly.
- Read the pass.

OBJECTIVE: Improving goalkeeper's game skills; communication, handling pressure and positioning

NUMBER OF PLAYERS: 12

AREA/FIELD: Half field

TIME: 15 - 20 minutes

EQUIPMENT: Two goals, 2 small goals, supply of balls

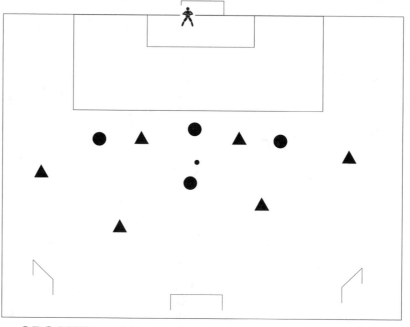

ORGANIZATION:
- Game of 6 v 4 on 2 goals with goalkeeper.
- Team of 6 puts pressure on goalkeeper with every backpass.
- Team of 4 can score on goal with goalkeeper, and goalkeeper can score on 2 small goals after backpass.

INSTRUCTIONS: Play full rules.

GOALKEEPING 14

COACHING POINTS:
- Communicate between goalkeeper and defense.
- Make backpass accurate and at right pace.

VARIATIONS: Play 6 v 6 or 4 v 4 plus 2 neutral players.

GOALKEEPING   15

OBJECTIVE: Improving stopping shots on goal

NUMBER OF PLAYERS: 7 - 12

AREA/FIELD: Half field

TIME: 15 - 20 minutes

EQUIPMENT: 3 cones, 1 goal, supply of balls

ORGANIZATION: Players take shots from 18 yard line after 1-2 combination with teammate.

INSTRUCTIONS:
• Let players switch position.
• All kinds of shots.

COACHING POINTS:
• Stay on toes, hands up.
• Keep eyes on ball.
• Cut off angles.

VARIATIONS: Introduce defenders.

GOALKEEPING 16

OBJECTIVE: Improving stopping shots on goal

NUMBER OF PLAYERS: 4 - 10

AREA/FIELD: Half field

TIME: 10 - 15 minutes

EQUIPMENT: 2 cones, 1 goal, supply of balls

ORGANIZATION: Goalkeeper throws or punts ball to player A who receives and dribbles towards goal. Defender puts pressure on player A. Player A can take shot on goal or he can lay the ball off to player B who shoots on goal.

INSTRUCTIONS: Let players shoot from outside 18 yard box.

COACHING POINTS:
- Move on line by goalkeeper.
- Communicate.
- Keep eyes on ball.
- Deflect shots to side.

GOALKEEPING   17

OBJECTIVE: Improving coming off line against break-a-ways

NUMBER OF PLAYERS: 8 - 12

AREA/FIELD: Half field

TIME: 15 - 20 minutes

EQUIPMENT: 4 cones, 1 goal, supply of balls

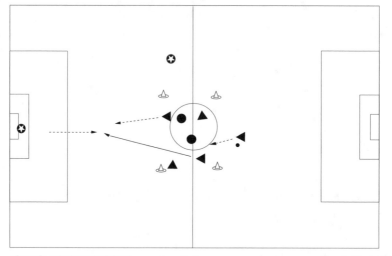

ORGANIZATION: 4 v 2 keep-away game at midfield. Coach calls out name or number of players. Ball is played into run of moving player for a 1 v 1 with goalkeeper.

INSTRUCTIONS:
- After player leaves grid, new player steps in and new 4 v 2 starts.
- Come off line quickly.
- Cut off angle.
- Stay low.
- Goalkeeper always ready to come and intercept pass or position in front of goal.

VARIATIONS: Introduce defender to put on pressure from behind.

GOALKEEPING 18

OBJECTIVE:	Improving coming off line against break-a-ways
NUMBER OF PLAYERS:	4 - 10
AREA/FIELD:	Half field
TIME:	10 - 15 minutes
EQUIPMENT:	1 goal, supply of balls

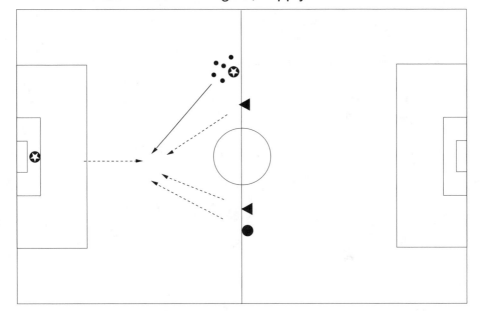

ORGANIZATION:	Coach plays ball into run of attacker going to goal. Extra defender and attacker start on opposite flank. Attacker tries to score with help of extra attacker.
INSTRUCTIONS:	Play ball into space between attacker and goalkeeper; 50/50 ball.
COACHING POINTS:	• Come off line quickly. • Judge pace and direction of ball. • Keep eye on ball but also on defender and attacker.

OBJECTIVE: Judging/recognizing through balls and improving play off line

NUMBER OF PLAYERS: 16

AREA/FIELD: Full field

TIME: 20 - 25 minutes

EQUIPMENT: 4 cones, 2 goals, supply of balls

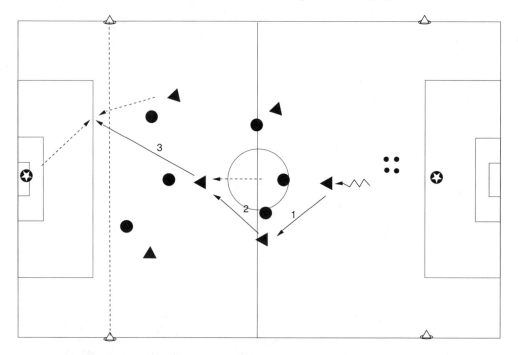

ORGANIZATION:
- 7 v 7 game (man to man, no sweeper).
- Defending team defends field in front of 20 yard line. Attacking team attempts to split defense or pass over top of defense into 20 yard zone and score on goal.

INSTRUCTIONS:
- Defenders cannot go past 20 yard line.

GOALKEEPING 19

- Attacking team may score from anywhere; Scoring after through pass or long pass counts double.
- Attacking team can't play combinations inside 20 yard zone.

COACHING POINTS:
- Goalkeeper must play off line.
- Communication between goalkeeper and defenders.
- Come off line quickly to intercept through pass.

GOALKEEPING

OBJECTIVE:	Improving 1 v 1 with attackers
NUMBER OF PLAYERS:	5 - 10
AREA/FIELD:	Third of field
TIME:	15 - 20 minutes
EQUIPMENT:	5 cones, 3 goals, supply of balls

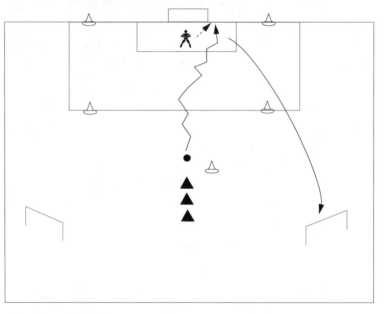

ORGANIZATION:	Attackers dribble toward goal and go 1 v 1 with goalkeeper.
INSTRUCTIONS:	• If goalkeeper wins ball he can score by punting or throwing ball into 1 of 2 goals. • Goalkeeper tries to force attacker outside zone (cones).
COACHING POINTS:	• Be patient. • Stay on feet as long as possible. • Cut off angles. • Stay low. • Force player to outside.

GOALKEEPING 21

OBJECTIVE: Improving 1 v 1 with attackers

NUMBER OF PLAYERS: 5 - 10

AREA/FIELD: Half field

TIME: 15 - 20 minutes

EQUIPMENT: 4 cones, 4 goals, supply of balls

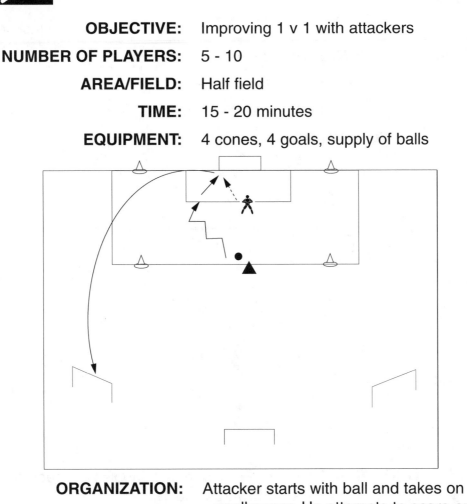

ORGANIZATION: Attacker starts with ball and takes on goalkeeper. He attempts to score on goal but cannot leave grid.

INSTRUCTIONS: When goalkeeper wins ball, he can score in 1 of 3 goals.

COACHING POINTS:
• Stay low, hands and feet ready.
• Force attacker to sides or back to midfield.
• Stay close to ball.
• Be patient, choose right moment to win ball.

GOALKEEPING   22

OBJECTIVE:	Improving 1 v 1 situations with attacker
NUMBER OF PLAYERS:	2 - 10
AREA/FIELD:	Third of field
TIME:	20 - 25 minutes
EQUIPMENT:	10 cones, 4 goals, supply of balls

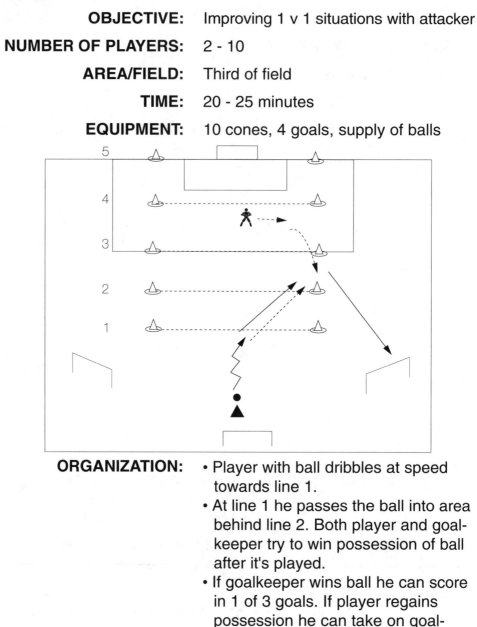

ORGANIZATION:	• Player with ball dribbles at speed towards line 1.
	• At line 1 he passes the ball into area behind line 2. Both player and goal-keeper try to win possession of ball after it's played.
	• If goalkeeper wins ball he can score in 1 of 3 goals. If player regains possession he can take on goal-keeper and try to score on goal.
INSTRUCTIONS:	Goalkeeper starts in area between lines 3 and 4.

GOALKEEPING 22

COACHING POINTS: • Read path and speed of ball.
• Make quick, smart decisions.
• Find new position quickly/footwork.

OBJECTIVE:	Improving 1 v 1 situations against break-a-ways.
NUMBER OF PLAYERS:	3 - 10 players
AREA/FIELD:	Third of field
TIME:	20 - 25 minutes
EQUIPMENT:	2 cones, 2 goals, supply of balls

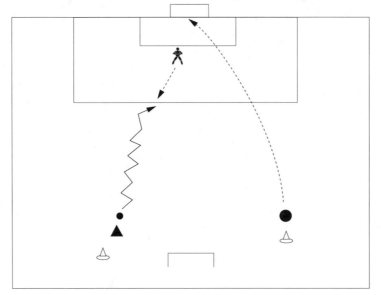

ORGANIZATION:	Player with ball is on break-a-way toward goal and tries to score. Goalkeeper comes off line and tries to stop attack, while defender makes a recovery run to cover goal. If defense wins possession, they can score in opposite goal.
INSTRUCTIONS:	Play at full game speed.
COACHING POINTS:	• Come off line and read situation.
	• Adjust position accordingly.
	• Communicate with defender.
	• Quick transition if ball is won.

OBJECTIVE:	Improving 1 v 1 situations with attacker
NUMBER OF PLAYERS:	3 - 10
AREA/FIELD:	Third of field
TIME:	20 - 25 minutes
EQUIPMENT:	1 cone, 4 goals, supply of balls

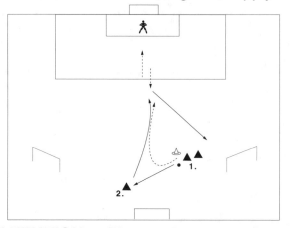

ORGANIZATION:	Player 1 passes to player 2 and makes a wide run. Player 2 passes the ball deep into player 1's run. Goalkeeper comes off line to take space in front of goal. Player 1 tries to score.
INSTRUCTIONS:	If goalkeeper wins ball he can score in 1 of 3 goals.
COACHING POINTS:	• Come off line and make attacker put his head down. • Read the flight of ball and make quick decisions. • Force player to outside or back to midfield. • Be ready to adjust and react.
VARIATIONS:	Vary trajectory of ball to player 1 (high, hard, to side, etc).

GOALKEEPING 25

OBJECTIVE: Improving 1 v 1 situations with attacker

NUMBER OF PLAYERS: 3 - 10

AREA/FIELD: Third of field

TIME: 20 - 25 minutes

EQUIPMENT: 1 cone, 4 goals, supply of balls

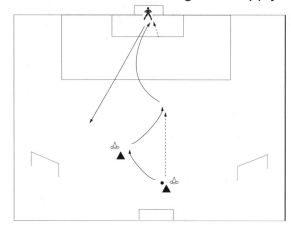

ORGANIZATION: Player 1 passes ball to player 2 and runs deep. Player 2 passes the ball deep into player 1's run. Goalkeeper comes off line to take space in front of goal. Player 1 tries to score.

INSTRUCTIONS: If goalkeeper wins ball he can score in 1 of 3 goals.

COACHING POINTS:
• Come off line and make attacker put his head down.
• Read the flight of ball and make quick decisions.
• Force player to outside or back to midfield.
• Be ready to adjust and react.

VARIATIONS: Vary trajectory of ball to player 1 (high, hard, to side, etc).

GOALKEEPING 26

OBJECTIVE:	Improving punching technique
NUMBER OF PLAYERS:	8 - 10
AREA/FIELD:	Third of field
TIME:	15 - 20 minutes
EQUIPMENT:	Supply of balls

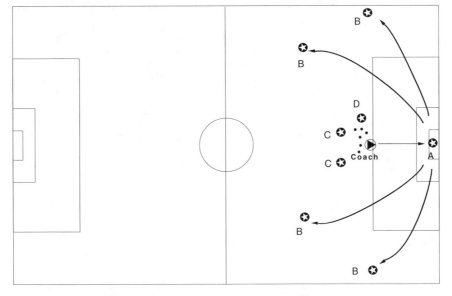

ORGANIZATION: Coach throws ball in air to goalkeeper in goal. Goalkeeper punches ball away to the sides.

INSTRUCTIONS:
• Four goalkeepers collect balls and throw them back to keepers C and D.
• Pressure goalkeeper.

COACHING POINTS:
• Punch ball at highest possible point.
• Call out, "keepers ball".
• Make fist to punch ball.
• Accurately punch ball to sides.

VARIATIONS: Let goalkeeper punch at targets (e.g. goals or moving players).

GOALKEEPING 27

OBJECTIVE:	Learning to intercept crosses from flanks
NUMBER OF PLAYERS:	12 - 14
AREA/FIELD:	Half field
TIME:	30 minutes
EQUIPMENT:	Five cones, 1 goal, supply of balls

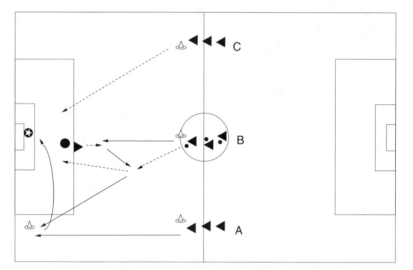

ORGANIZATION:	• Player B passes ball to player on top of 18 yard box (under pressure of defender). Player wallpasses and player B passes to player A on flank. Player A crosses ball to player B and C. • Goalkeeper tries to intercept cross.
INSTRUCTIONS:	• Cross from left and right. • In and outswinging crosses.
COACHING POINTS:	• Follow the whole play. • Communicate with defender. • Position of line, side ways on. • Catch cross at highest possible point. • In a "ready position" at all times.

GOALKEEPING 27

VARIATIONS: Let goalkeeper, if he wins ball, restart game by throwing at target.

GOALKEEPING 28

OBJECTIVE:	Improving handling of crosses from flank
NUMBER OF PLAYERS:	3 - 6
AREA/FIELD:	Third of field
TIME:	15 - 20 minutes
EQUIPMENT:	2 cones, supply of balls

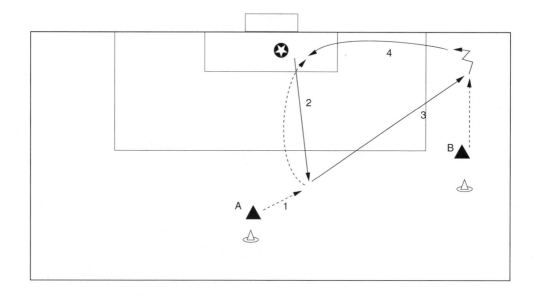

ORGANIZATION:	Goalkeeper throws ball to player A. Player A gives a pass to Player B on flank. Player B crosses ball and goalkeeper intercepts/catches cross. Player A goes to goal to try to score.
INSTRUCTIONS:	Vary crosses from left and right.
COACHING POINTS:	• Read flight of ball. • Call for ball. • Catch at highest possible point.

GOALKEEPING 29

OBJECTIVE:	Improving handling of crosses from flank outside 18 yard box
NUMBER OF PLAYERS:	4 - 8
AREA/FIELD:	Third of field
TIME:	15 - 20 minutes
EQUIPMENT:	3 cones, supply of balls

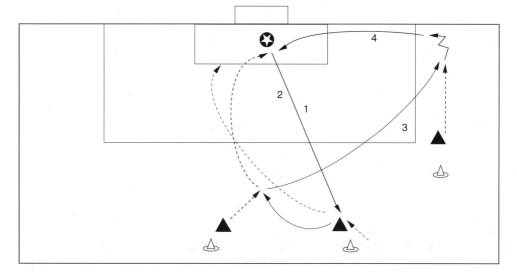

ORGANIZATION:	Goalkeeper throws out ball to player 1. Player 1 passes ball to player 2 who passes ball to player 3 on flank. Players 1 and 2 make runs in front of goal and try to finish cross on goal. Goalkeeper tries to intercept cross.
INSTRUCTIONS:	• Vary crosses. • From left and right side flank.
COACHING POINTS:	• Follow whole play. • Read flight of ball. • Call for ball. • Catch ball at highest point.

GOALKEEPING 30

OBJECTIVE: Improving handling of crosses from flank

NUMBER OF PLAYERS: 6 - 10

AREA/FIELD: Half field

TIME: 20 - 25 minutes

EQUIPMENT: 4 cones, 2 goals, supply of balls

ORGANIZATION: Goalkeeper throws ball to player A. Player A passes ball to player B who passes wide to player C. Player C crosses ball in front of goal. Goalkeeper catches ball and restarts game the same way.

INSTRUCTIONS:
• Pass wide to left and right to get crosses from both sides of field.
• Defender pressures player A. If defender wins ball he can score on goal at midfield.

COACHING POINTS:
• Make accurate throws/passs by Goalkeeper.
• Come off line to catch cross.
• Call for ball.

OBJECTIVE:	• Improving intercepting crosses
	• Improving quick distribution
	• Improving defending against break-a-ways
NUMBER OF PLAYERS:	12 - 16 players
AREA/FIELD:	Full field
TIME:	30 minutes
EQUIPMENT:	Supply of balls

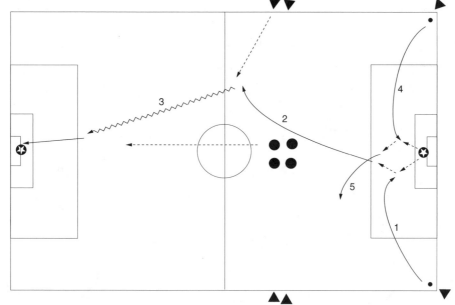

ORGANIZATION: Player takes a corner kick. Goalkeeper catches cross and throws or punts ball to player on side at midfield. Player receives ball and runs with ball toward opposite goal to take on goalkeeper. Extra defender puts pressure on attacker from behind.

INSTRUCTIONS: Alternate sides (left and right corners).

GOALKEEPING

COACHING POINTS:
- Distribute quickly after catching ball.
- Utilize accurate punting or throwing.
- Slow down attacker to wait for support from defender.
- Force attacker to side.

VARIATIONS: Start game on two sides of field at same time.

GOALKEEPING   32

OBJECTIVE:	Improving game coaching by goalkeeper
NUMBER OF PLAYERS:	7
AREA/FIELD:	Half field
TIME:	30 minutes
EQUIPMENT:	3 cones, 2 goals, supply of balls

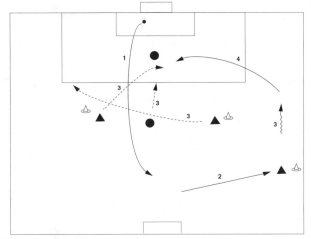

ORGANIZATION: Goalkeeper throws or punts ball to other side of field. Player receives ball and passes it to player on flank. Player on flank receives and dribbles toward end line before crossing into box. Attckers try to score under pressure of 2 defenders.

INSTRUCTIONS: Goalkeeper coaches his defense and tries to win back ball or stop opposition from scoring. When defense wins ball they can score in goal at midfield.

COACHING POINTS: • Organize defense quickly.
• Stay organized.
• Communicate.
• Make quick transition.

GOALKEEPING 33

OBJECTIVE: Improving situation related coaching by goalkeeper and defense

NUMBER OF PLAYERS: 12 players

AREA/FIELD: Half field

TIME: 30 minutes

EQUIPMENT: 2 cones, 2 goals, supply of balls

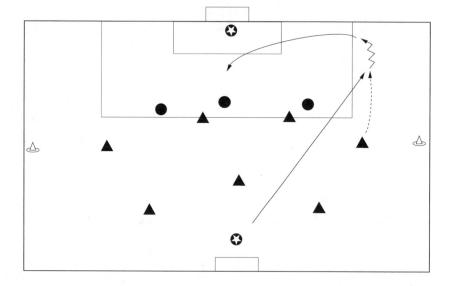

ORGANIZATION: Game of 7 v 3 plus 2 goalkeepers.

Team of 7 tries to score. Team of 3 plus goalkeeper organizes defense and tries to win back ball.

INSTRUCTIONS:
• Game starts with goalkeeper of team of 7 with ball.
• When defense wins ball they can score in goal at midfield.

COACHING POINTS:
• Communicate, clear and specific.
• Know players' responsibilities.
• Keep defense compact.

GOALKEEPING 34

OBJECTIVE:	Improving handling crosses from flank and coaching game situations
NUMBER OF PLAYERS:	12
AREA/FIELD:	Three-fourths of field
TIME:	30 minutes
EQUIPMENT:	2 cones, supply of balls

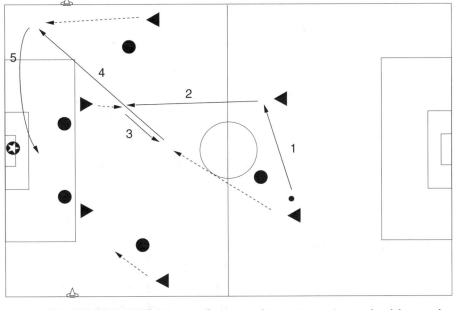

ORGANIZATION:	• Game of 6 v 5 on 1 goal with goal-keeper. • Team of 6 tries to build up over flank and score in goal with goalkeeper.
INSTRUCTIONS:	Goalkeeper plus team of 5 organizes defense and tries to stop opposition from scoring and win back ball.
COACHING POINTS:	• Communicate, clear and specific. • Know players' responsibilities. • Keep defense compact and together.

OBJECTIVE:	Learning to intercept crosses in game situations
NUMBER OF PLAYERS:	14
AREA/FIELD:	Two-thirds of field
TIME:	30 minutes
EQUIPMENT:	2 cones, 2 goals, supply of balls

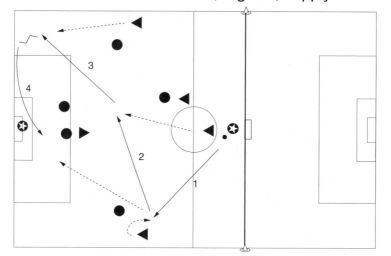

ORGANIZATION: Game of 6 v 6 on 2/3 of field. Both teams play a 2-2-1 formation to create a numerical advantage on offense to create build-up over the flanks (more crosses).

INSTRUCTIONS:
- Both teams attempt to score on goal with goalkeeper.
- Encourage crosses and build-up over flanks.

COACHING POINTS:
- Keep defense organized and aware.
- Play game-like.
- Coach defenders (when, where, how and what).
- Know responsibilities.

Chapter 7

CONDITIONING

CONDITIONING 1

OBJECTIVE:	Improving reaction time, speed and acceleration
NUMBER OF PLAYERS:	14 - 18
AREA/FIELD:	Half field
TIME:	10 minutes
EQUIPMENT:	4 cones, 1 ball

ORGANIZATION:	Coach throws up ball to 2 players who challenge each other in the air. If ball ends up on the side of the B players, they will chase the players on the A side.
INSTRUCTIONS:	B players will try to tag the A players before they pass the line between the 2 cones.
COACHING POINTS:	React quickly. Sharp acceleration.
VARIATIONS:	Instead of heading challenge, shot on goal.

CONDITIONING 2

OBJECTIVE:	Improving reaction and acceleration
NUMBER OF PLAYERS:	10 - 14
AREA/FIELD:	2 grids of 10 yards x 20 yards
TIME:	10 minutes
EQUIPMENT:	8 cones, 10 flags, ball per player

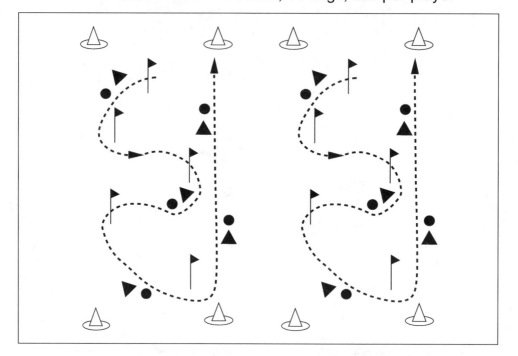

ORGANIZATION:	Players dribble through course inside grid (players stay behind each other). On signal they leave their ball, sprint around the next ball and continue the course with third ball.
INSTRUCTIONS:	Keep correct spacing between players.
COACHING POINTS:	Dribble at game speed.
VARIATIONS:	Let players sprint around next ball and turn back to own ball.

CONDITIONING 3

OBJECTIVE: Improving stamina, speed

NUMBER OF PLAYERS: 1 - 14

AREA/FIELD: 20 yards x 60 yards

TIME: 10 minutes

EQUIPMENT: 8 cones

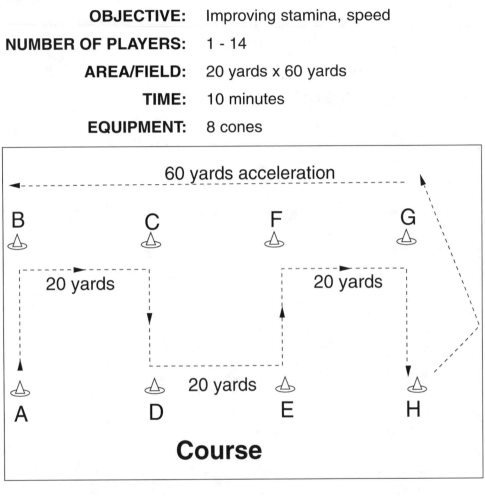

Course

ORGANIZATION: Players sprint from A to B, from B to C, etc.

INSTRUCTIONS:
- Keep enough space between players.
- Let players sprint, hop, skip etc. from cone to cone.

CONDITIONING

4

OBJECTIVE:	Improving reaction and acceleration
NUMBER OF PLAYERS:	Groups of 3
TIME:	10 minutes
EQUIPMENT:	1 ball per 3 players

ORGANIZATION:	• Player B dribbles ball while players A and C jog alongside him. • On signal player B passes ball into space. All 3 players try to win ball.
INSTRUCTIONS:	Alternate players after 5 passes.
COACHING POINTS:	• React quickly to pass. • Always stay on toes.
VARIATIONS:	Let player juggle and volley ball away.

CONDITIONING 5

OBJECTIVE:	Improving reaction and acceleration
NUMBER OF PLAYERS:	4 - 12
AREA/FIELD:	Grid 30 yards x 30 yards
TIME:	10 minutes
EQUIPMENT:	5 cones

D   C

X2

X1

A   B

ORGANIZATION:	• Players 1 and 2 start jogging toward cone in middle of grid. • Player 1 fakes and sprints away toward outside of grid. Player 2 follows and tries to beat player 1.
INSTRUCTIONS:	Get close to cone in middle before faking.
COACHING POINTS:	Keep eyes on player.
VARIATIONS:	Use ball and dribble to cone in middle.

CONDITIONING 6

OBJECTIVE:	Improving starting and sprinting with and without ball
NUMBER OF PLAYERS:	10 - 15
AREA/FIELD:	Grids 10 yards x 30 yards
TIME:	10 - 15 minutes
EQUIPMENT:	10 cones, 1 ball

ORGANIZATION:	• Grid 1: Player A passes ball to player B and follows ball by sprint. Player B receives ball and dribbles to middle. In middle player B passes ball to player C and follows ball with sprint.
	• Grid 2: Player 1 sprints from 1 to 2, 2-3, etc.
	• Player sprinting goes around each cone.
INSTRUCTIONS:	Perform everything at full speed.
VARIATIONS:	Use 2 balls simultaneously.

CONDITIONING 7

OBJECTIVE:	Improving reaction speed
NUMBER OF PLAYERS:	4 - 10
TIME:	10 minutes
EQUIPMENT:	2 cones, 3 small goals, supply of balls

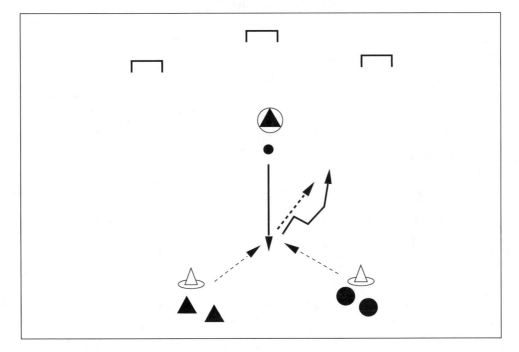

ORGANIZATION:	Coach plays ball in front of 2 players. Both players sprint to ball. They will try to win ball and score in one of 3 goals.
COACHING POINTS:	Score as quick as possible.
VARIATIONS:	Let players start from various positions: e.g. push-up position, face up, face down.

CONDITIONING 8

OBJECTIVE:	Improving sprinting speed, stamina, and passing at high speed
NUMBER OF PLAYERS:	Groups of 3
TIME:	10 minutes
EQUIPMENT:	1 ball per 3 players

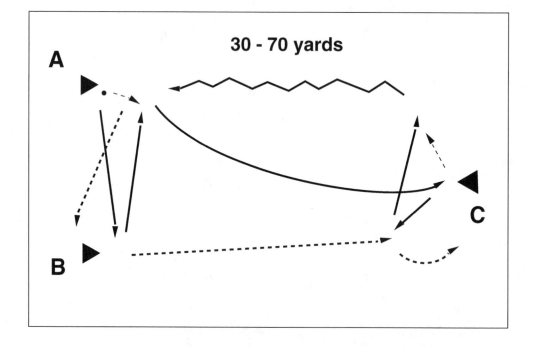

ORGANIZATION:	Players A and B play a 1-2 combination. Player A opens with long pass to player C. Player B follows pass with sprint. Player B and C play a 1-2 combination and Player C dribbles to A position.
INSTRUCTIONS:	Players rotates as follows: A to B, B to C, C to A.
COACHING POINTS:	Make accurate, hard passes.

CONDITIONING 9

OBJECTIVE:	• Improving speed/sprints • Scoring from cross
NUMBER OF PLAYERS:	5 - 15
AREA/FIELD:	Half field
TIME:	15 minutes
EQUIPMENT:	5 gates/hurdles, 5 cones, supply of balls

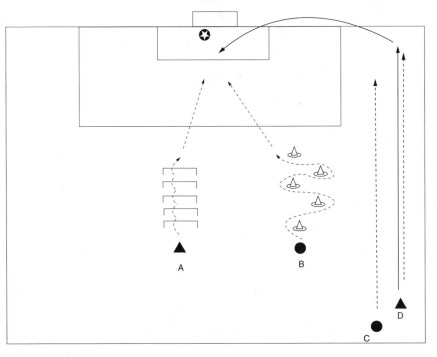

ORGANIZATION:	• Players A and B go over/through obstacles. Player D plays a long ball into space. Player D goes after pass and tries to score. • Player C goes after player D and tries to prevent player D from crossing. Players A and B finish cross.
INSTRUCTIONS:	Let players alternate positions.

OBJECTIVE: • Improving starting speed/sprints
• Finish crosses under pressure

NUMBER OF PLAYERS: 8 - 16

AREA/FIELD: Half field

TIME: 15 minutes

EQUIPMENT: 7 cones, supply of balls

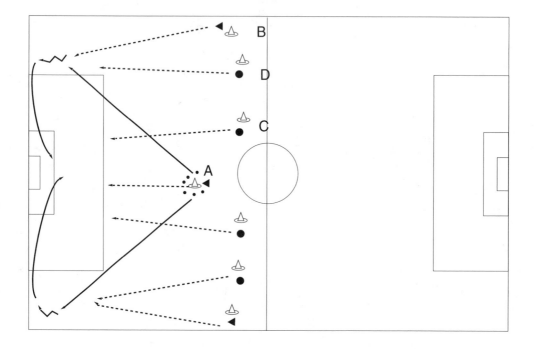

ORGANIZATION: Player A plays ball to flank to player B. Player B tries to cross ball under pressure of player D. Defender C defends player A who tries to finish cross.

INSTRUCTIONS: Let players alternate sides and switch positions.

CONDITIONING 11

OBJECTIVE:	Improving starting and sprinting speed
NUMBER OF PLAYERS:	12
AREA/FIELD:	Full field
TIME:	15 minutes
EQUIPMENT:	2 cones

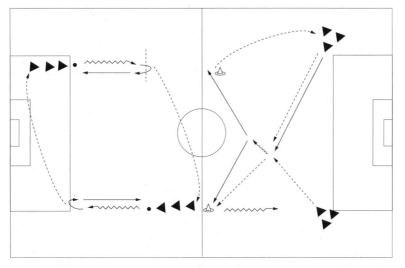

ORGANIZATION: **A:** Player dribbles with ball for approximately 20 yards, turns quickly, passes ball back to next player and sprint to other group on other side.

B: Player 1 passes ball into run of player 2. Player 1 follows pass and overlaps player 2. Player 2 passes ball into run of player 1. Player 1 finishes drill by dribbling around cone back to starting position. Player 2 sprints round other cone and back to start.

INSTRUCTIONS: Everything at game speed.

CONDITIONING   12

OBJECTIVE:	Improving sprinting in challenge for ball
NUMBER OF PLAYERS:	6 - 12 players
AREA/FIELD:	Full field
TIME:	15 minutes
EQUIPMENT:	8 cones, supply of ball

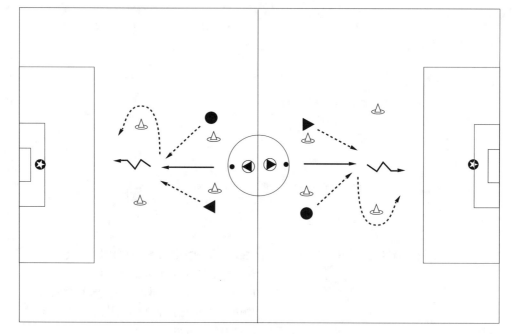

ORGANIZATION: Coach passes ball into space in front of 2 players. Both players try to win ball. The player with ball goes on to shoot on goal. Player without ball sprints around and then tries to stop other player from scoring.

COACHING POINTS:
• In possession of ball, take shortest route to goal.
• Use game-like offense and defense.

OBJECTIVE:	Improving stamina using game situations
NUMBER OF PLAYERS:	12 - 16
AREA/FIELD:	Full field
TIME:	15 minutes
EQUIPMENT:	11 cones, supply of balls

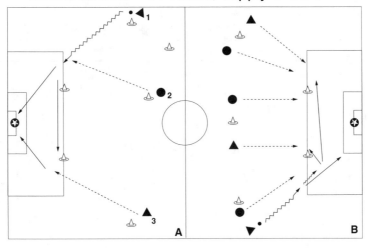

ORGANIZATION: A: Player 1 dribbles at full speed under pressure of player 2 towards 18 yard box. At 18 line he decides to shoot or play ball to player 3 who shoots on goal.

B: Player 1 dribbles under pressure of defender to 18 yard box. Inside 18 yard box he decides to shoot or lay ball off to 1 of 2 teammates (pressured by defenders), who shoots at goal.

INSTRUCTIONS: Game-like execution.

COACHING POINTS:
• Choose shortest route to goal.
• Play with head up.

CONDITIONING

OBJECTIVE:	Improving stamina and fitness using game situations
NUMBER OF PLAYERS:	18 - 20
AREA/FIELD:	Full field
TIME:	30 minutes
EQUIPMENT:	8 cones, supply of balls

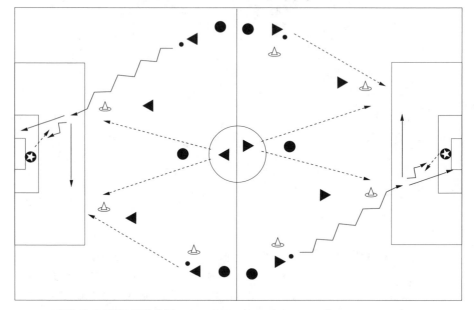

ORGANIZATION:	Player on flank runs with ball toward 18 yard box. He is pressured by defender. From midfield 2 more attackers and defenders make a run down field. Player with ball has option to finish ball himself or pass ball to one of teammates to finish.
INSTRUCTIONS:	Game-like execution.
COACHING POINTS:	• Play with head up. • Execute at full speed. • Score.

CONDITIONING 15

OBJECTIVE:	Improving fitness (stations)
NUMBER OF PLAYERS:	20
AREA/FIELD:	Full field
TIME:	Two minutes per station, 30 second break between stations
EQUIPMENT:	4 cones, 5 flags, supply of balls

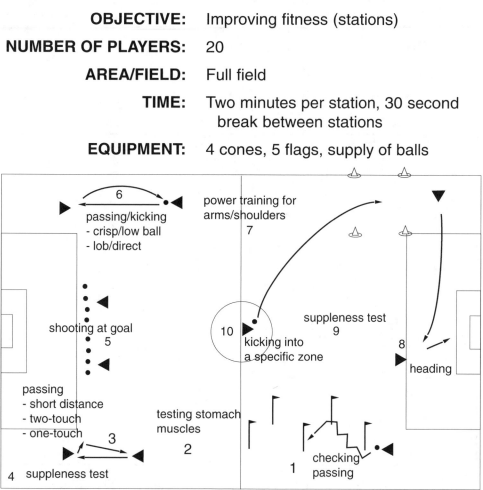

ORGANIZATION:	Two players per station. Players go around and perform specific drill per station. • (suppleness test = stretching) • (power training = push-ups) • (testing stomach = sit-ups)
INSTRUCTIONS:	Let players move from station quickly.
COACHING POINTS:	Concentration and effort at each station.

CONDITIONING

16

OBJECTIVE:	Improving stamina using passing drill
NUMBER OF PLAYERS:	Groups of 4
TIME:	10 minutes
EQUIPMENT:	1 ball per 4 players

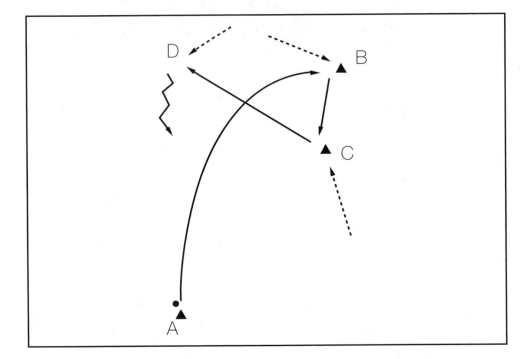

ORGANIZATION:	Player A plays a long ball to player B. B plays ball short to C who passes to D. D receives ball and dribbles to starting position at speed.
INSTRUCTIONS:	All players rotate positions.
COACHING POINTS:	• Make accurate passes. • Execute at high speed. • Follow pass by sprint.
VARIATIONS:	Introduce defender.

CONDITIONING 17

OBJECTIVE:	Improving stamina using passing drill
NUMBER OF PLAYERS:	3 - 6
AREA/FIELD:	20 yards x 40 yards
TIME:	10 minutes
EQUIPMENT:	4 cones, 2 balls

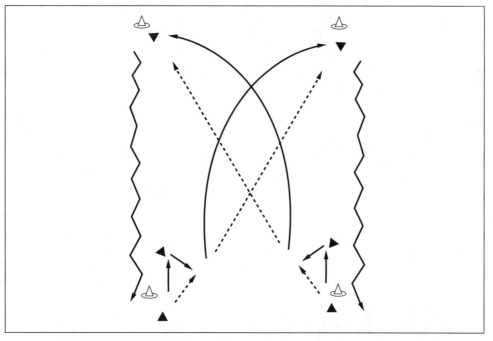

ORGANIZATION:
- Players 1 and 2 play short combination. Player 1 receives ball and plays a long diagonal ball to player 3 on other side of grid.
- Player 3 dribbles back to starting position.

INSTRUCTIONS:
- Player 1 follows ball by sprint.
- Players rotate in position.

COACHING POINTS: Make accurate passes.
Sprint right after pass.

CONDITIONING   18

OBJECTIVE: Interval training (passing)

NUMBER OF PLAYERS: Groups of 4

AREA/FIELD: Approximately 40 yards x 30 yards

TIME: 16 minutes (each player 4 minutes in circle)

EQUIPMENT: 2 balls per 4 players

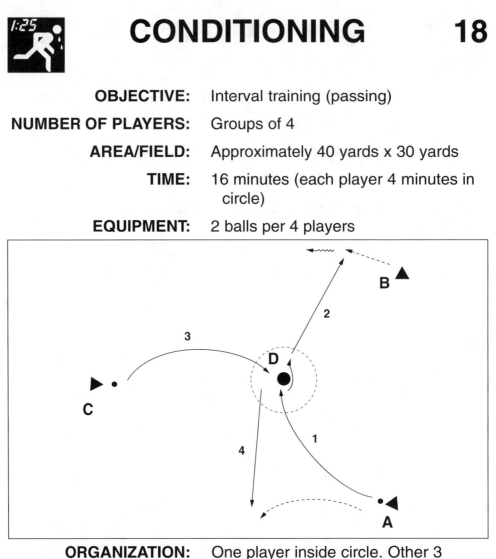

ORGANIZATION: One player inside circle. Other 3 players spread out around circle (20 yard distance). One player with ball passes a long ball to player in middle. Player in middle receives ball and passes it to player without ball.

INSTRUCTIONS: Give player in middle little time between passes.

COACHING POINTS:
• Practice accurate passing.
• Player receiving (middle and outside) always moving.

CONDITIONING 19

OBJECTIVE:	Interval training (passing)
NUMBER OF PLAYERS:	Groups of 3
AREA/FIELD:	Grids 10 yards x 30 yards
TIME:	12 minutes
EQUIPMENT:	4 cones, 1 ball per grid

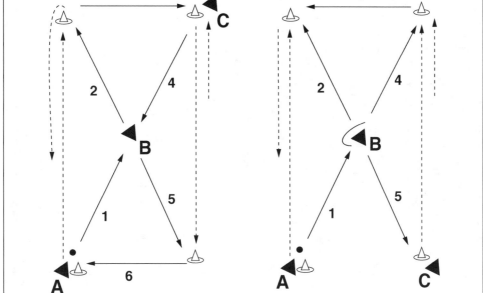

ORGANIZATION:	• Player A passes ball to player B in middle of grid. • After pass player A sprints to open corner. Player B turns and passes to player A or plays one touch to player C.
INSTRUCTIONS:	Keep ball and players always moving.
COACHING POINTS:	Make accurate passes. Concentrate. Communicate.

CONDITIONING

OBJECTIVE:	Interval training (sprints)
NUMBER OF PLAYERS:	8 - 20
AREA/FIELD:	Full field
TIME:	15 minutes
EQUIPMENT:	10 cones

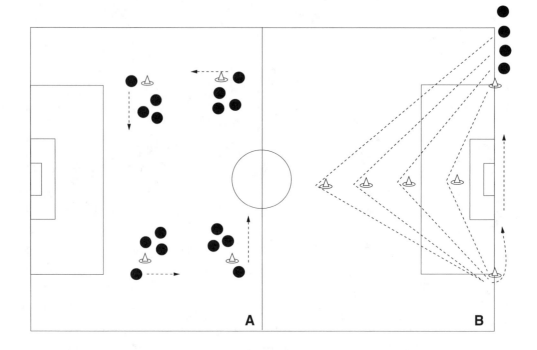

ORGANIZATION:	A. Players sprint around grid.
	B. Players sprint around cone to other side of 18 yard box.
COACHING POINTS:	Make quick turns.

CONDITIONING

OBJECTIVE:	Interval training with ball
NUMBER OF PLAYERS:	4 - 16
AREA/FIELD:	Full field
TIME:	15 minutes
EQUIPMENT:	10 cones, supply of balls

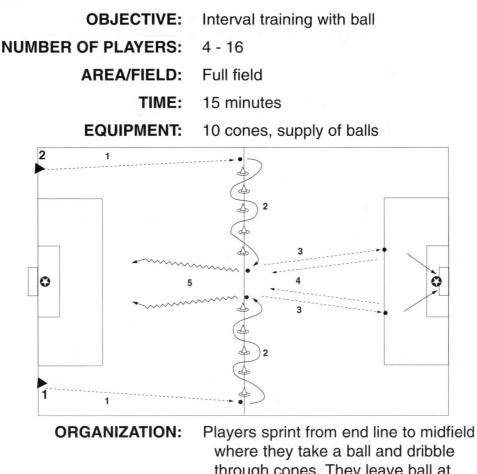

ORGANIZATION:	Players sprint from end line to midfield where they take a ball and dribble through cones. They leave ball at end of dribbling course and sprint to 18 yard line and shoot a ball at goal. After shot they sprint back to midfield and dribble ball to opposite 18 yard box and shoot ball on goal.
INSTRUCTIONS:	Let 2 players start at same time.
COACHING POINTS:	Dribble as fast as possible without losing control.
VARIATIONS:	Let players compete against each other.

CONDITIONING

OBJECTIVE:	Interval training
NUMBER OF PLAYERS:	6 - 16
AREA/FIELD:	Full field
TIME:	15 minutes
EQUIPMENT:	9 cones, 3 hurdles, 2 balls

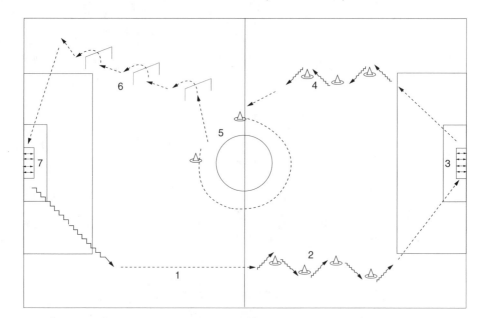

ORGANIZATION: Player starts at goal. He jumps to touch cross bar 4 times and sprints to midfield. He takes a ball and dribbles through cones. Leave ball at last cone and sprint to goal. Four jumps to touch crossbar and sprint to dribbling course. Dribble through cones and leave ball at last cone. Sprint around the center circle, sprint to hurdles (hop on 2 legs) and finish with sprint to goal.

INSTRUCTIONS: Everything at high speed.

OBJECTIVE:	Improving stamina in passing drill
NUMBER OF PLAYERS:	10
AREA/FIELD:	30 yards x 30 yards
TIME:	15 minutes
EQUIPMENT:	1 ball

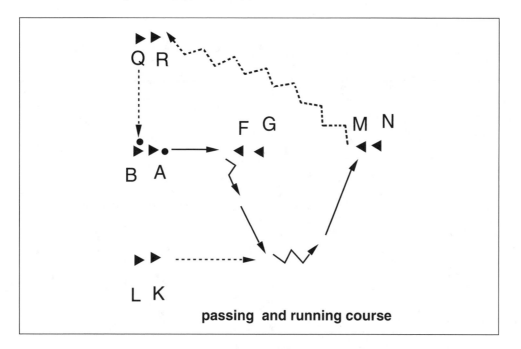

passing and running course

ORGANIZATION:
- Player A passes to player F. Player F turns with ball and passes into player K's run.
- Player K dribbles and passes ball to player M who dribbles to player Q.
- Player Q passes to player B.
- Each player that passes sprints to follow their pass to next station.

INSTRUCTIONS: Alternate sides.

COACHING POINTS: Accurate passing and quick movement.

CONDITIONING 24

OBJECTIVE:	Interval training (shooting)
NUMBER OF PLAYERS:	12 - 18
AREA/FIELD:	Full field
TIME:	20 minutes
EQUIPMENT:	4 goals, supply of balls

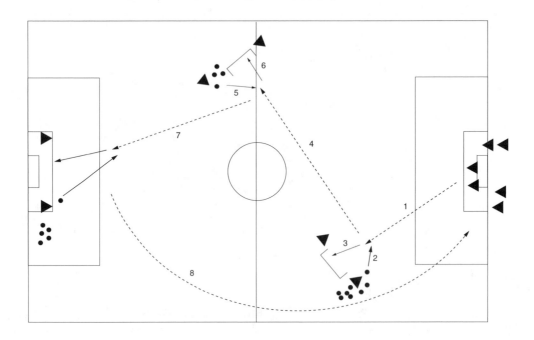

ORGANIZATION: Player 1 starts at goal and sprints toward next goal where he receives a pass and shoots on goal. After shot he sprints to next goal and repeats.

INSTRUCTIONS: After player 1 has taken first shot, next player 2 can start drill.

COACHING POINTS: Concentrate on shooting even when fatigued.

VARIATIONS: Let defender put pressure on attacker.

CONDITIONING   25

OBJECTIVE:	Improving fitness in passing drill
NUMBER OF PLAYERS:	6 - 12 players
AREA/FIELD:	Half of field
TIME:	10 - 15 minutes
EQUIPMENT:	supply of balls

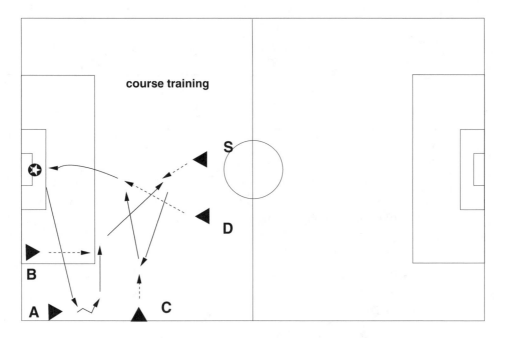

course training

ORGANIZATION:	Goalkeeper throws ball out to player A. A dribbles and passes in B's run. Player B passes ball to S who plays 1 touch to player C (start from side line). Player C passes ball into run of D who finishes with shot on goal.
COACHING POINTS:	• Concentrate on accurate passing. • Play 1 touch as much as possible. • Keep ball on ground.
VARIATIONS:	Ball 1 touch.

CONDITIONING   26

OBJECTIVE:	Improving stamina/fitness with ball
NUMBER OF PLAYERS:	16 - 20 players
AREA/FIELD:	Full field
TIME:	15 minutes
EQUIPMENT:	Supply of balls

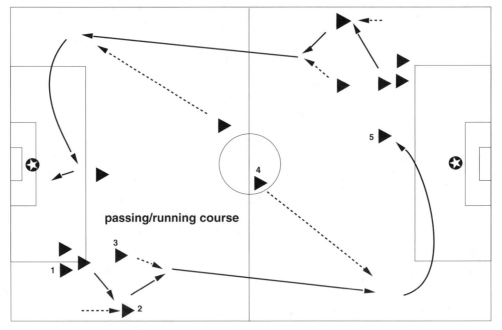

passing/running course

ORGANIZATION:	Players 1, 2 and 3 play a quick combination. Player 3 plays a long ball into player 4's run (Start from midfield). Player 4 receives ball and crosses ball to player 5 who finishes on goal.
INSTRUCTIONS:	• Let both sides start at same time. • Goalkeeper in goals.
COACHING POINTS:	• Communicate. • Make passes into runs.
VARIATIONS:	Introduce defenders.

CONDITIONING

OBJECTIVE:	Interval training (stations)
NUMBER OF PLAYERS:	6 - 12 players
AREA/FIELD:	Half of field
TIME:	20 minutes
EQUIPMENT:	11 cones, 2 hurdles, 2 goals, supply of balls

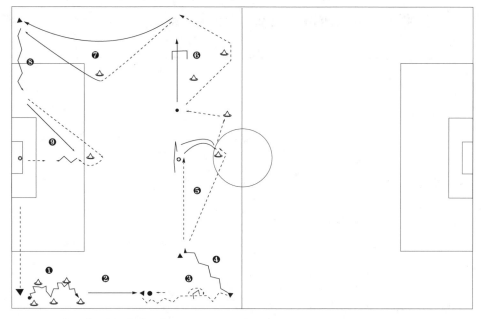

ORGANIZATION: Players go through stations. Start at goal and finish with shot on goal.
1. Dribbling.
2. Pass to teammate, sprint to receive return pass, turn away from defender and accelerate away with ball.
3. Pass through gate/hurdle.
4. Dribble and pass to goalkeeper.
5. Sprint around cone and head ball lobbed from goalkeeper on goal.

6. Sprint to cone, collect ball and pass through gate/hurdle and run around cone to regain ball.

7. Long pass to corner and sprint around cone.

8. Fast dribble, pass to cone.

9. Sprint around cone, collect ball and take on goalkeeper 1 v 1.

INSTRUCTIONS: Exercise can start at different stations at same time.

CONDITIONING

OBJECTIVE: Improving stamina and fitness in passing drill

NUMBER OF PLAYERS: 10 - 15

AREA/FIELD: Half of field

TIME: 15 minutes

EQUIPMENT: 4 hurdles/Dutch gates, supply of balls

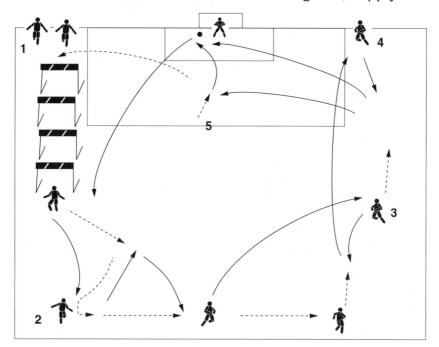

ORGANIZATION:
- Player 1 starts with jump over hurdles. Goalkeeper throws ball into run and plays a double 1-2 combination. Player 2 plays long ball to player 3 on the flank and moves to open space.
- Player 3 passes the ball back, first time to player 2.
- Player 2 plays a long ball to player 4 in corner. Player 4 plays ball back to

INSTRUCTIONS: player 3 who crosses ball to player in front of goal to player 5 who shoots.

COACHING POINTS:
- Let player know exactly where to go after every pass.
- Players move up 1 position.

- Communicate.
- Make accurate passes.
- Put enough pace on ball.

CONDITIONING

OBJECTIVE:	Interval training
NUMBER OF PLAYERS:	12 - 18
AREA/FIELD:	Full field
TIME:	15 minutes
EQUIPMENT:	4 cones, supply of balls

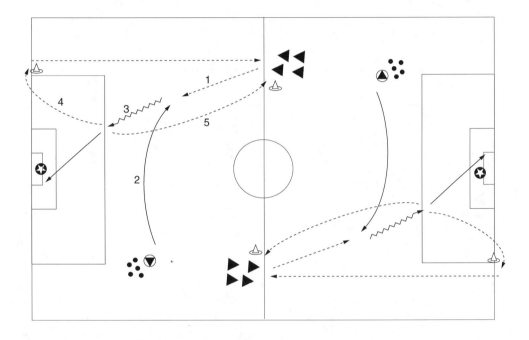

ORGANIZATION:	Player sprints toward 18 yard box and receives pass by coach. Dribbles to top of 18 yard line and shoots on goal. After shot, sprints around cone and back to starting position.
INSTRUCTIONS:	Second players start as soon as first player has taken shot.

OBJECTIVE:	Interval training
NUMBER OF PLAYERS:	9 - 15
AREA/FIELD:	Full field
TIME:	15 minutes
EQUIPMENT:	9 cones, supply of balls

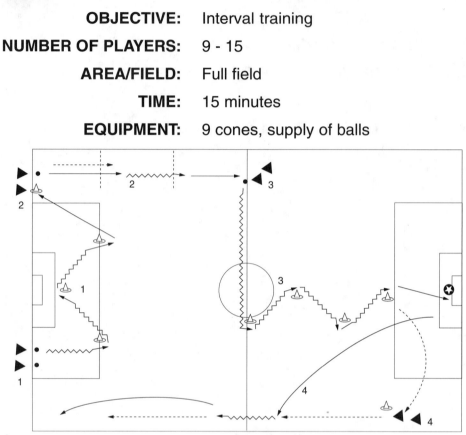

ORGANIZATION: Player 1 dribbles around cones. At last cone he passes to player 2 and follows pass. Player 2 passes ball into space and sprints to regain possession and passes to player 3, who dribbles around cones from center circle to 18 yard line and shoots. After shot sprint to position of player 4. Goalkeeper throws ball into run of player 4 who receives, dribbles and passes ball to starting position.

INSTRUCTIONS: Next player starts when player 1 rounds last cone.

CONDITIONING 31

OBJECTIVE: Interval training

NUMBER OF PLAYERS: 8 - 12

AREA/FIELD: Three-fourths of field

TIME: 15 minutes

EQUIPMENT: 11 cones, 2 goals, supply of balls

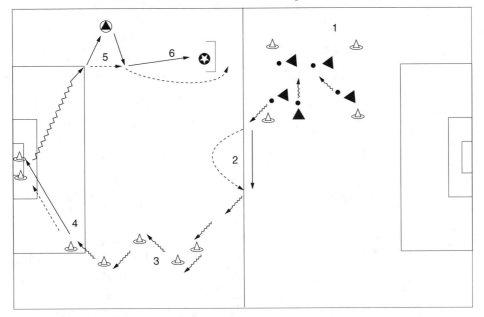

ORGANIZATION:
- Players dribble inside grid. When number is called, player dribbles to the center circle.
- Pass ball to other side of circle and sprint around circle. Collect ball and dribble through cones. At last cone pass ball to cones in goal mouth and follow pass with sprint.
- Collect ball and pass to coach. Coach will play 1-2 combination. Finish with shot on goal.

COACHING POINTS: Everything at game speed.

OBJECTIVE: Improving fitness in game situation

NUMBER OF PLAYERS: 8 - 14

AREA/FIELD: Full field

TIME: 15 minutes

EQUIPMENT: Supply of balls

ORGANIZATION: A. Player 1 plays a 1-2 combination with player 2 and player 3. Player 3 plays ball to player 2 who passes to the cones for player 3 to run onto and cross ball to teammates inside box.

B. Player 1 plays a long ball to player 2 (under pressure of defender). After pass player 1 makes overlapping run. Player 2 receives ball and turns toward goal and plays ball into player 1's run. Player 1 crosses ball to teammates inside box. Player 2 sprints to position 1 and player 1 to position 2.

COACHING POINTS:
• Runs/overlaps at full speed.
• Play ball at right time.

CONDITIONING   33

OBJECTIVE:	Fitness training stations
NUMBER OF PLAYERS:	15 - 20 players
AREA/FIELD:	Full field
TIME:	15 minutes
EQUIPMENT:	9 cones, supply of balls

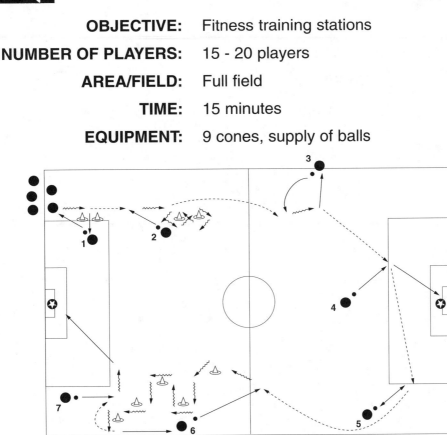

ORGANIZATION: Player goes through stations.
1. Sprint, 1-2 combination.
2. Receive pass and dribble around cones, pass ball back and sprint.
3. 1-2 combination, sprint to station 4.
4. Receive and shoot first time.
5. Sprint, 1-2 combination.
6. Receive pass and dribble around cones, pass back to player.
7. Receive ball, dribble and shoot at goal.

INSTRUCTIONS: After going through stations, switch with feeder at a station.

CONDITIONING 34

OBJECTIVE:	Improving stamina
NUMBER OF PLAYERS:	6 - 12
AREA/FIELD:	Full field
TIME:	15 minutes
EQUIPMENT:	3 cones, supply of balls

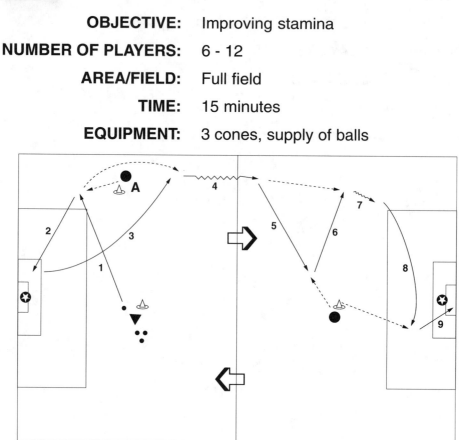

ORGANIZATION: • Receive pass from feeder and play ball back to goalkeeper. Sprint around cone and receive pass back from goalkeeper. Dribble and pass ball to teammate showing for ball. Play long 1-2 combination.
• Receive pass and cross to teammate who finishes on goal.

INSTRUCTIONS: After cross, switch with player who shoots on goal.

COACHING POINTS: • Accurate combinations.
• Quick movements into space.

CONDITIONING 35

OBJECTIVE: Improving stamina using shooting exercises

NUMBER OF PLAYERS: 14 - 20 players

AREA/FIELD: Full field

TIME: 5 - 10 minutes per station

EQUIPMENT: 10 cones, supply of balls

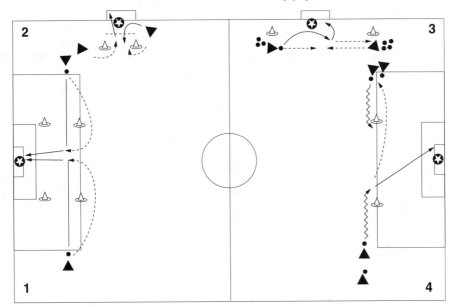

ORGANIZATION:
- Station 1: Pass to self, sprint around cone and shoot at goal.
- Station 2: Pass to teammate who sprints around cone and shoots at goal.
- Station 3: Pass in air to teammate who shoots at goal.
- Station 4: Dribble around cone, shot on goal and sprint to other side.

INSTRUCTIONS: Players switch after 5 to 10 minutes at each station.

OBJECTIVE: Improving stamina/fitness in stations

NUMBER OF PLAYERS: Groups of 3 or 4 per station

AREA/FIELD: Full field

TIME: Five minutes per station

EQUIPMENT: 8 cones, supply of balls

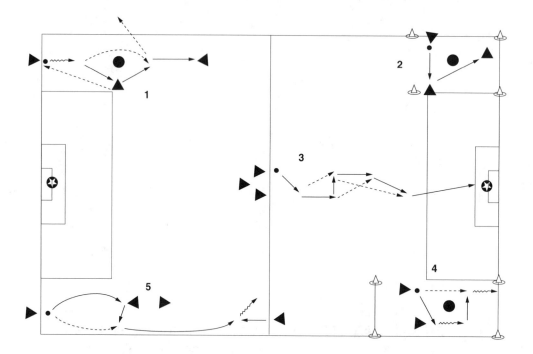

ORGANIZATION:
1. 1-2 combination in rotation.
2. 3 v 1 keep-away.
3. 1-2 combinations to finish on goal.
4. 2 v 1 (score by dribbling over line).
5. Throw in, wallpass, long 1-2 combination.

INSTRUCTIONS: Players switch after 5 minutes at each station.

OBJECTIVE: Improving stamina using passing and dribbling

NUMBER OF PLAYERS: 3 players per station

AREA/FIELD: Full field

TIME: 4 minutes per station

EQUIPMENT: 4 cones, supply of balls

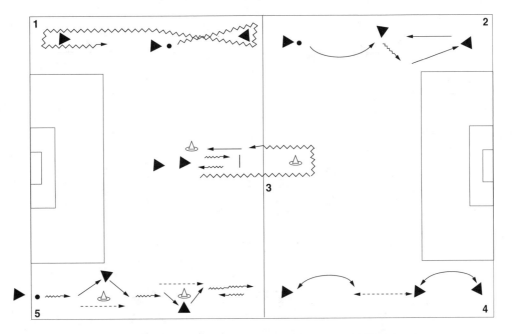

ORGANIZATION:
- Station 1: Dribbling around teammates in figure eight.
- Station 2: Passing-receiving 180 turn, pass.
- Station 3: Dribble to line, turn, back to cone, turn, dribble around cone.
- Station 4: Player in middle heads ball back to teammates on outside.
- Station 5: 1-2 combination around cones.

CONDITIONING 38

OBJECTIVE: Improving stamina/fitness in stations

NUMBER OF PLAYERS: Groups of 4

TIME: 6 minutes per station

EQUIPMENT: 14 cones, supply of balls

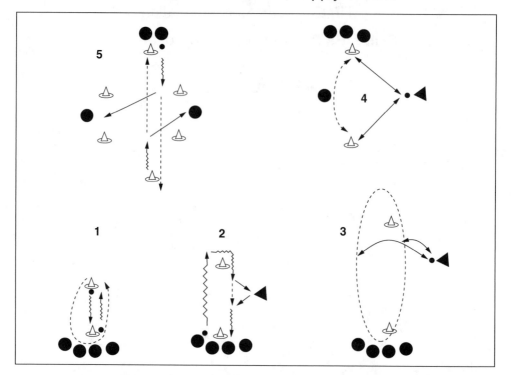

ORGANIZATION:
- Station 1: Dribble to cone, sprint without ball around both cones, collect ball and dribble back.
- Station 2: Dribbling, 1-2 combination.
- Station 3: Sprint around cones, head ball.
- Station 4: Sprint, pass to feeder.
- Station 5: Dribble, pass ball to teammate, finish with sprint.

INSTRUCTIONS: Groups switch stations after 6 minutes.

OBJECTIVE: Interval training in stations

NUMBER OF PLAYERS: 12 - 24

AREA/FIELD: Full field

TIME: 4 minutes per station

EQUIPMENT: 12 cones, 5 flags, 2 boards, 6 hurdles/ Dutch gates, supply of balls

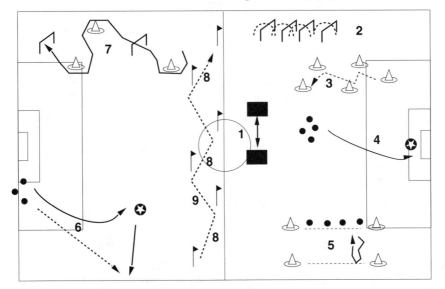

ORGANIZATION:

- Station 1: Pass against board (1 touch).
- Station 2: Jump over hurdles.
- Station 3: Sprint to cones (quick turns).
- Station 4: Consecutive shots on goal.
- Station 5: Dribble ball to other side of grid, leave and sprint back to collect next ball.
- Station 6: Play long 1-2 combination.
- Station 7: Dribble around cones (short turns) and pass through gates.
- Station 8/9: Sprint/jog.

CONDITIONING 40

OBJECTIVE:	Interval training (2 v 1)
NUMBER OF PLAYERS:	10 - 14
AREA/FIELD:	25 yards x 25 yards
TIME:	15 minutes
EQUIPMENT:	6 cones, supply of balls

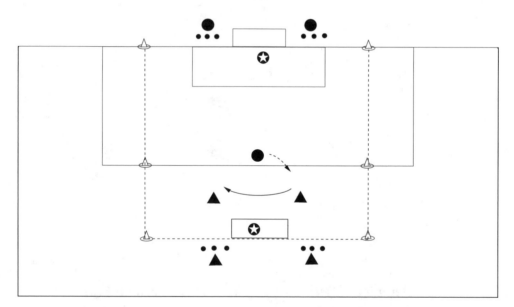

ORGANIZATION:	2 v 1 in grid. 2 attackers try to score on goal with goalkeeper.
INSTRUCTIONS:	Two attackers get ball from feeders on side of goals. After the ball has been shot they get new ball from feeders. Work for 4 minutes.
COACHING POINTS:	• Shoot quickly but don't rush attack. • Play/pass with pace. • Communication between defender and goalkeeper. • Defender force attack wide.

CONDITIONING

OBJECTIVE:	Improving fitness in game situation
NUMBER OF PLAYERS:	16
AREA/FIELD:	50 yards x 60 yards
TIME:	10 - 15 minutes
EQUIPMENT:	4 cones, supply of balls

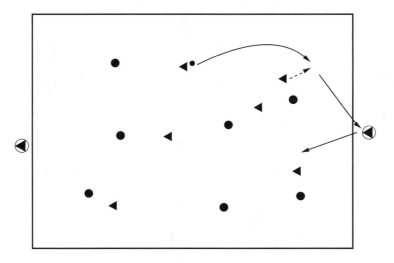

ORGANIZATION:	Two teams (plus 2 neutral players) play 7 v 7 keep away.
INSTRUCTIONS:	If team wins back possession, they must use opposite neutral player before they can use other neutral player. Neutral players have 1 touch.
COACHING POINTS:	• Spread out defense. • Play ball accurately. • Communicate. • Use numerical advantage.
VARIATIONS:	Use 4 neutral players.

CONDITIONING

OBJECTIVE:	Improving fitness in game situations.
NUMBER OF PLAYERS:	8 - 10
AREA/FIELD:	40 yards x 50 yards
TIME:	10 - 15 minutes
EQUIPMENT:	8 cones, supply of balls

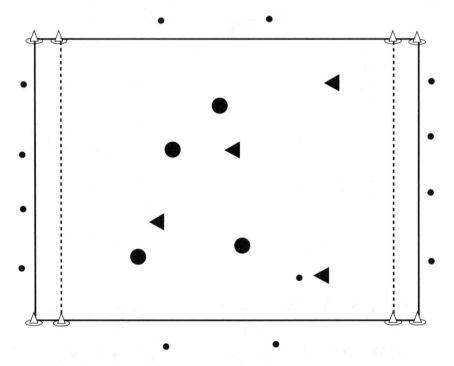

ORGANIZATION:	Teams score by dribbling ball over line and stopping ball inside zone at end of field.
INSTRUCTIONS:	Put plenty of extra balls at every end to ensure constant play.
COACHING POINTS:	• Spread out defense. • Take on defenders close to line. • Play two touch or one touch.

OBJECTIVE: Interval training 1 v 1

NUMBER OF PLAYERS: 6

AREA/FIELD: 15 yards x 35 yards

TIME: 4 minutes per pair

EQUIPMENT: 8 cones, supply of balls

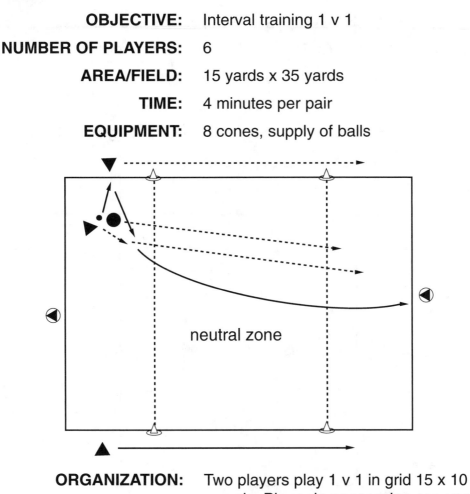

neutral zone

ORGANIZATION: Two players play 1 v 1 in grid 15 x 10 yards. Player in possession can use 3 neutral players on outside of grid. He may also switch grids by using long pass to other side of field. The 2 neutral players on side of grid move with player to create 3 v 1 again.

INSTRUCTIONS: Neutral players have 1 touch.

COACHING POINTS:
• Use whole grid.
• Correct pace and direction on pass to neutral players.

CONDITIONING 44

OBJECTIVE:	Improving fitness and stamina
NUMBER OF PLAYERS:	12 players plus goalkeeper
AREA/FIELD:	30 yards x 55 yards
TIME:	20 minutes
EQUIPMENT:	8 cones, 4 flags, supply of balls

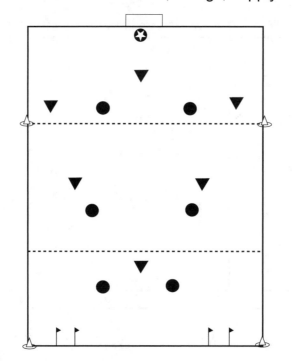

ORGANIZATION:
- Two teams of 6 players. The field is divided into thirds. The game starts with goalkeeper.
- Defending team has a 3 v 2 situation and tries to get ball into middle third where there becomes a 4 v 4 situation. The 4 players in the middle third attempt to get ball in final third where

they create a 2 v 2 situation (1 midfielder moves to final third) and they attempt to score on one of the two small goals.

INSTRUCTIONS: When opposition wins ball they can score in goal with goalkeeper.

COACHING POINTS: Exploit numerical advantage in defending third and play ball at right time.

CONDITIONING 45

OBJECTIVE:	Improving stamina in game situation
NUMBER OF PLAYERS:	12 plus goalkeeper
AREA/FIELD:	30 yards x 40 yards (10 yards x 40 yards on flanks)
TIME:	5 minute games
EQUIPMENT:	8 cones, supply of balls

ORGANIZATION:	2 v 2. Team in possession can use flank players for wallpass, or flank player can take on defender and cross the ball back to 2 teammates.
INSTRUCTIONS:	Flank players can't score.
COACHING POINTS:	When ball is played to flank player, make run away from ball but also a run to create an option for flank player.
VARIATIONS:	Try to score quickly.

CONDITIONING 46

OBJECTIVE:	Improving stamina and fitness in game situations
NUMBER OF PLAYERS:	14 plus 2 goalkeepers
AREA/FIELD:	• Field 40 yards x 50 yards • Neutral zone in front of goal 15 yards x 30 yards • Neutral zone on flanks 10 yards wide
TIME:	20 minutes
EQUIPMENT:	12 cones, supply of balls

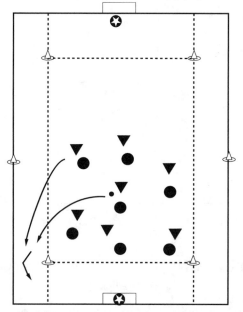

ORGANIZATION:	Two teams play 7 v 7 in field 40 x 50 yards. They have the opportunity to use neutral zones to cross ball from or to score from. Defending team is not allowed in neutral zones.
INSTRUCTIONS:	Two touch in neutral zones.
COACHING POINTS:	Play ball into zones at right time. Make runs into zone at right time.

CONDITIONING 47

OBJECTIVE:	Interval training 1 v 1
NUMBER OF PLAYERS:	6
AREA/FIELD:	20 yards x 30 yards
TIME:	3 minutes per series
EQUIPMENT:	4 cones, supply of balls

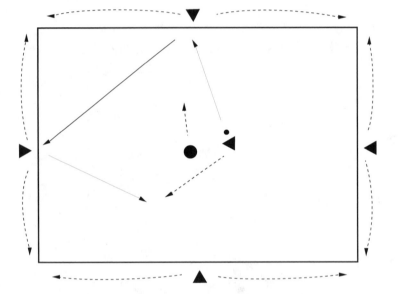

ORGANIZATION:	1 v 1 with 4 neutral players to play wallpasses.
INSTRUCTIONS:	• Neutral players only have one touch. • Switch 1 v 1 after every 3 minutes.
COACHING POINTS:	• After pass to neutral player, immediate movement to create option. • Play with head up. • Neutral players are moving. • Correct pace and accuracy of pass.
VARIATIONS:	2 v 2 plus 4 neutral players.

CONDITIONING

48

OBJECTIVE:	Improving stamina and scoring
NUMBER OF PLAYERS:	14
AREA/FIELD:	35 yards x 45 yards
TIME:	15 minutes
EQUIPMENT:	2 goals, supply of balls

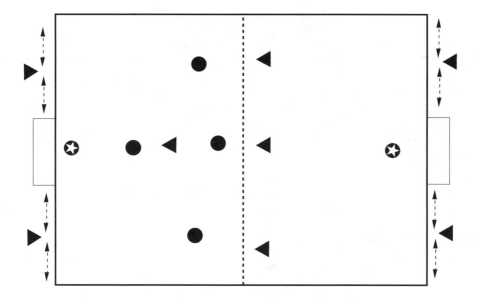

ORGANIZATION:	• 4 v 4 plus goalkeeper plus 2 wallpassers on each side. • Players can score only after pass from wallpasser on side of goal.
INSTRUCTIONS:	Play restrictions; 2 touch.
COACHING POINTS:	• Everything at game speed; quick movement, quick shooting. • Create 6 v 4 situations. • Communicate.
VARIATIONS:	Play one touch.

OBJECTIVE:	Improving stamina through 4 v 2
NUMBER OF PLAYERS:	8
AREA/FIELD:	20 yards x 40 yards
TIME:	10 - 15 minutes
EQUIPMENT:	6 cones, 1 ball

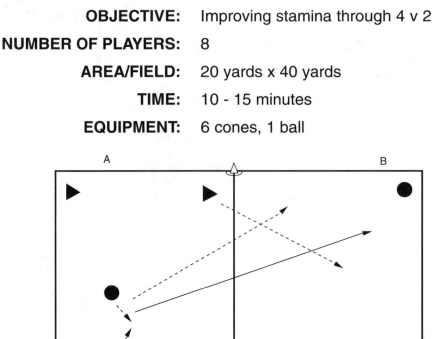

ORGANIZATION:	• 4 v 2 keep-away in grid 20 x 20 yards. • Four attackers try to keep possession. When 2 defenders win ball they play ball quickly to teammates in adjacent grid and play 4 v 2.
INSTRUCTIONS:	Two attackers become defenders in other grid after losing possession.
COACHING POINTS:	• Ten consecutive passes is point. • Transition and runs are at full speed. • Quick and intelligent movement on offense and defense.

OBJECTIVE: Conditioning through small-sided games

NUMBER OF PLAYERS: 8

AREA/FIELD: 2 grids of 15 yards x 5 yards

TIME: 10 minutes

EQUIPMENT: 8 Cones, 1 ball

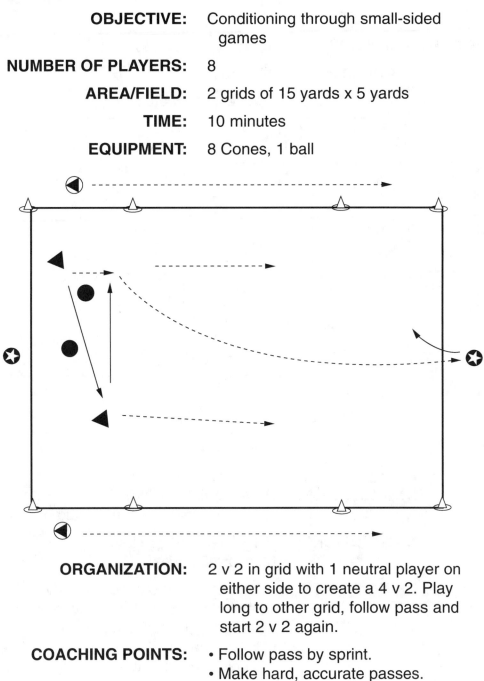

ORGANIZATION: 2 v 2 in grid with 1 neutral player on either side to create a 4 v 2. Play long to other grid, follow pass and start 2 v 2 again.

COACHING POINTS:
• Follow pass by sprint.
• Make hard, accurate passes.

CONDITIONING 51

OBJECTIVE:	Measuring sprint speed
NUMBER OF PLAYERS:	1 - 10
AREA/FIELD:	10 yards
EQUIPMENT:	4 cones, stopwatch

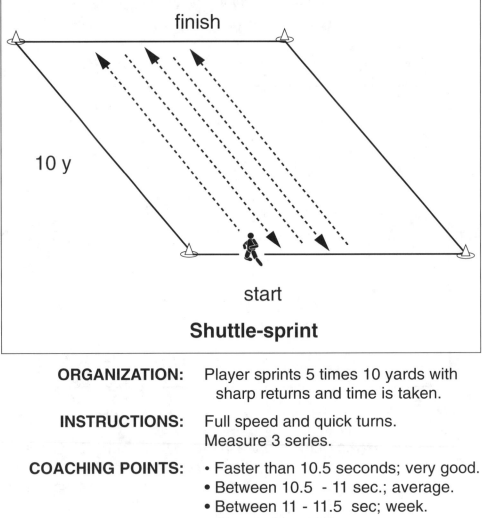

Shuttle-sprint

ORGANIZATION:	Player sprints 5 times 10 yards with sharp returns and time is taken.
INSTRUCTIONS:	Full speed and quick turns. Measure 3 series.
COACHING POINTS:	• Faster than 10.5 seconds; very good.
	• Between 10.5 - 11 sec.; average.
	• Between 11 - 11.5 sec; week.
	• Slower than 11.5 sec ; poor.
	• Accelerate out of turns.

CONDITIONING

OBJECTIVE:	Measuring speed and stamina
NUMBER OF PLAYERS:	1 - 10
AREA/FIELD:	50 yards
EQUIPMENT:	12 cones, stopwatch

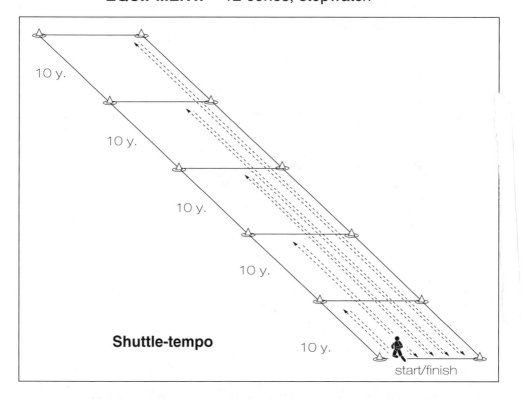

Shuttle-tempo

start/finish

ORGANIZATION:	Players run from start back and forth to 10, 20, 30, 40, 50 yard line (i.e 300 yards).
INSTRUCTIONS:	Go full speed from start to finish.
COACHING POINTS:	• Less than 57 seconds; very good.
	• Between 57 - 60 sec; average.
	• Between 60 - 63 sec; below average.
	• Slower then 63 seconds; poor.
	• Accelerate out of turns.

CONDITIONING 53

OBJECTIVE:	Measuring stamina, shuttle run test
NUMBER OF PLAYERS:	6 - 16
AREA/FIELD:	20 yards x 26 yards
TIME:	5 minutes
EQUIPMENT:	8 cones

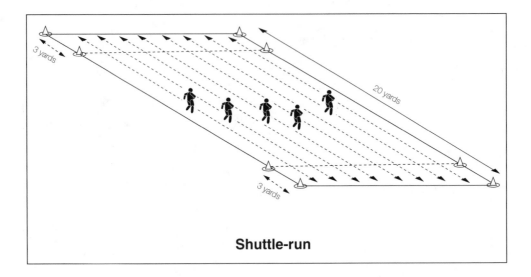

Shuttle-run

ORGANIZATION:	Players run from one side of grid to other.
INSTRUCTIONS:	• Jog 3 yards, accelerate hard and sprint 20 yards. • Five second interval and go again. • Repeat 10 times.
COACHING POINTS:	• Acceleration. • Use arms and bring knees up. • Sprint through 20 yard line.

CONDITIONING 54

OBJECTIVE: Conditioning while shooting at goal

NUMBER OF PLAYERS: 2- 10

AREA/FIELD: Third of field

TIME: 10 - 15 minutes

EQUIPMENT: 2 goals, supply of balls

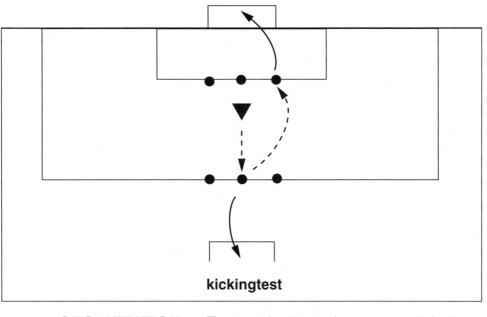

kickingtest

ORGANIZATION: Two goals 20 yards apart. 6-10 balls are placed on 6 and 18 yard line. Player shoots balls into empty goals as quickly as possible going from 6 to 18 yard line and back.

INSTRUCTIONS: Let player decide sequence.

COACHING POINTS: • Sprint until all balls are shot on goal.
• Don't slow down to shoot.

VARIATIONS: Extra task for missed shots e.g. push ups, sprints, etc.